HEINRICH ZIMMER

HEINRICH ZIMMER

COMING INTO HIS OWN

Margaret H. Case,

Editor

PRINCETON UNIVERSITY PRESS

PRINCETON, NEW JERSEY

LIBRARY OF CONGRESS CATALOGING-IN-PUBLICATION DATA

HEINRICH ZIMMER : COMING INTO HIS OWN / EDITED BY

MARGARET H. CASE.

P.   CM.

AND INDEX.

ISBN 0-691-03337-4

1. ZIMMER, HEINRICH ROBERT.   1890–1943—CONGRESSES.

2. INDIA—CIVILIZATION—CONGRESSES.   3. INDOLOGISTS—

GERMANY—BIOGRAPHY—CONGRESSES.   I. CASE, MARGARET H.

DS435.7.Z56H45   1994

954.03′5—DC20   93-29645

THIS BOOK HAS BEEN COMPOSED IN ADOBE PALATINO

PRINCETON UNIVERSITY PRESS BOOKS ARE PRINTED

ON ACID-FREE PAPER AND MEET THE GUIDELINES FOR

PERMANENCE AND DURABILITY OF THE COMMITTEE ON

PRODUCTION GUIDELINES FOR BOOK LONGEVITY

OF THE COUNCIL ON LIBRARY RESOURCES

PRINTED IN THE UNITED STATES OF AMERICA

1   3   5   7   9   10   8   6   4   2

CONTENTS

LIST OF ILLUSTRATIONS

*Unless otherwise noted, all photographs are from the
collection of the Zimmer family.*

HEINRICH ZIMMER

INTRODUCTION

Margaret H. Case

THIS VOLUME has grown out of a conference held on December 6, 1990 that marked the hundredth anniversary of Heinrich Zimmer's birth.[1] Zimmer's works in English—*Myths and Symbols in Indian Art and Civilization, Philosophies of India, The Art of Indian Asia, The King and the Corpse, Artistic Form and Yoga in the Sacred Images of India*—have inspired several generations of students of Indian religion and culture. Zimmer wrote about India with a feeling and an understanding rarely found among Western scholars. It is those qualities that attract first-time readers, and that continue to inspire even those who quarrel with some of his interpretations. And yet there is often some reservation in the enthusiasm of those who speak of his work. For one thing, it is not always clear how much of what appears under his name is in fact his own. At the time of his sudden and untimely death, most of his ideas were in the form of rough drafts and lecture notes, and the corpus that now exists in English under his name was largely stitched together by others, most notably by his student Joseph Campbell. Campbell relied on the "two bins of notes and papers" Zimmer left behind[2]—and, as Wendy Doniger points out in her essay in this volume, on the voice of Zimmer recollected or recreated. Although "this arduous piece of editorial craftsmanship" was, as A. K. Coomaraswamy wrote, "unselfishly and very skilfully carried out,"[3] it leaves open the question of where Zimmer ends and Campbell begins in these volumes, a question Wendy Doniger explores in her essay. Because Campbell is more highly esteemed among the general public than among academics, Zimmer's reputation among scholars has suffered. In addition, the intellectual and philosophical influence of C. G. Jung on Zimmer in the last years of his life—and his growing influence on Campbell during the 1950s—has raised questions of whether Zimmer's work became hostage to Jung's depth psychology. As Jung's

---

[1] The conference was sponsored by the Southern Asian Institute of Columbia University.

[2] Joseph Campbell, "Editor's Foreword" to Heinrich Zimmer, *Myths and Symbols in Indian Art and Civilization*, ed. Joseph Campbell, Bollingen Series VI (New York: Pantheon, 1946), v.

[3] A. K. Coomaraswamy, review of Zimmer, *Myths and Symbols in Indian Art and Civilization* in *Review of Religion* 11, no. 3 (March 1947): 285.

writings attract criticism from many quarters, Zimmer's "Jungianism" is also implicated.

There is another factor in the uneasiness about Zimmer's legacy, which can be traced to his own marginal position in the academic profession during his lifetime. As will be evident from the papers in this volume, Zimmer did not find his intellectual companionship among run-of-the mill academics, and his admirers and supporters were not academic Sanskritists or Indologists, either in Germany or later in America. Since Zimmer's erudition was widely acknowledged, we may ask why he was never fully accepted by the academic establishment. For one thing, his career was interrupted by four years of military service in World War I—an experience that pushed him to escape from the confines of traditional academic endeavor. Partly for this reason, he was ahead of his time in embracing cross-disciplinary studies, and in his essay Gerald Chapple documents the irritation he caused scholars who defined their field of study more narrowly. Exacerbating this tension, Zimmer was exuberant by nature, and not shy about expressing his enthusiasms and dislikes. Not everyone was charmed by his personality; some found him overbearing and arrogant. Prominent among his dislikes were those he considered narrow-minded intellectuals—including his teacher, Heinrich Lüders. Again, Chapple presents evidence of the price Zimmer paid for his impatience with them.

Those of Zimmer's works that were edited by Joseph Campbell, long available in English, are frequently recommended and read in America as introductions to Indian studies. Although they resonate with a life and vitality that cannot be matched, because of their Jungianism (and their Campbellianism) many of these books are not taken seriously, however, except as introductions. But in his first and most original work, *Kunstform und Yoga im indischen Kultbild*, only recently available in English as *Artistic Form and Yoga in the Sacred Images of India*,[4] Zimmer's ideas are, by the consensus of the papers gathered here, worthy of more serious consideration. Here, as in the German works as yet untranslated and a few short pieces in English also published without Campbell's editing, Zimmer speaks for himself.[5]

There is an irony in our quest to find the "real" Zimmer, since he spent much of his life doing just that. The "real" Zimmer seemed to be inextricably mixed with a vision of the "real" India—a country Zimmer never visited except in his imagination. Yet when he spoke or

[4] *Artistic Form and Yoga in the Sacred Images of India*, trans. Gerald Chapple and James B. Lawson in collaboration with J. Michael McKnight (Princeton: Princeton University Press, 1984).

[5] For a useful overview these publications, see the "Selected Bibliography of Zimmer's Works," on pp. 261–67 of *Artistic Form and Yoga*.

wrote about this India he had constructed in his mind, his words carried a greater sense that it was a living civilization than did those of most Western scholars who had traveled or even studied there. How could this have been so?

As his daughter, Maya Rauch, testifies, Zimmer's life and his learning were not separate, and he pursued both with vigor and passion. He believed that the Indian material he studied—sacred art and esoteric texts—contained material from a real world, a world he found more engaging than those created by his academic colleagues. Shortly before his death he wrote:

> Imagining India, its dense deep fragrance in my nostrils, the jungle before me, unknown, perhaps unknowable, I thought of this southern sky of which I had read: studded with strange stars and bewildering asterisms: none of them familiar to us; and yet a whole civilization, many civilizations, had steered their boats looking up and orientating themselves from this totally different pattern. Life worked as well the other way round, and it was worth while embarking for this other ocean.[6]

Although he never literally embarked for India, Zimmer related what he was learning about India to his own life, and because his studies were rooted in his experience of living, his writings on India also carried a sense of life and truth.

Zimmer found Western scholars of India deficient on two grounds: pedants by nature or training, they failed to relate philological findings to human questions; and, faced with ideas and images they did not understand, they dismissed them as false or worthless on the basis of their own cultural assumptions. Although Zimmer rebelled against the narrowness of his teachers' and colleagues' judgments, he knew that their assumptions lay at the core of his own culture and therefore of his own understanding. He knew his external life to be bound by European culture, and he was as scornful of attempts by Westerners to adopt the forms of Indian life without understanding what lay behind them as he was of "the sterilizing anatomy and dehydration of the merely intellectual approach of sheer scientist-philologists."[7] In his appreciation of the Indian material, therefore, he was always in dialogue with Western paradigms—especially challenging the deeply rooted conviction that their norms were superior to any others.

What was it that he was looking for in the Indian texts and sacred images? The papers by Matthew Kapstein and Mary Linda point us to the roots of his search in the German romantic tradition, which found

---

[6] Heinrich Zimmer, "Some Biographical Remarks about Henry R. Zimmer," appendix ibid., 248.

[7] Ibid., 258.

intellectual analyses of the type that dominated European academic circles unsatisfactory. "The current representation of India," wrote Zimmer in his brief memoir, "lacked color, intensity, consistency, life. For years I was in search of the 'real' India, of 'my' India, of Schopenhauer's India."[8] Kapstein points out the similarity between Schopenhauer's understanding of the "will" and Zimmer's interpretation of *shakti*, the fundamental energy that underlies all life, in Tantric doctrine. The "real" India for which Zimmer searched, then, was one that took account of the energy of life as he understood it, and so lived not in his imagination alone but at the intersection of the physical and the spiritual worlds, where the understanding of one depended on knowledge of the other.

This is the world he recreated in his first book, *Kunstform und Yoga im indischen Kultbild*, published in 1926. "I did not write it for professionals, nor as a contribution to specialized studies. I had to write it, to realize my self and to come into my own."[9] In this book, and in the brief autobiography reprinted with the English translation, we can glimpse his method of study: keen observation and rigorous self-confrontation. "An understanding of any art," Zimmer wrote, "requires that we bring our first impression into unprejudiced focus, that we be honest enough not to skim over any one part of our impression."[10] Suggesting in us the possibility that we would share these impressions with him if we were as sensitive and as honest as he was, he draws us into an understanding that is not based solely on accumulated information or intellectual reconstruction of a distant time and place. He asks us, rather, to become aware of alternative ways of seeing and knowing, ways we are not used to acknowledging. Thus his writing seems fresh even when details of fact or interpretation have been overturned by later research.

The impetus that enabled Zimmer to shed the academic straitjacket was his military service during the First World War—"four years of human, sub- and superhuman experience, initiations in the trenches, staffs, meeting more people than I ever did before and watching them in all kinds of revealing attitudes. The initiation of Life (including

---

[8] Ibid., 258–59.

[9] Ibid., 255.

[10] *Artistic Form and Yoga*, 6. Zimmer wrote that he had always been interested in art "to such a degree that both of my parents expected me to take up history of modern art as my major field of university studies. But I felt, during my first terms, not sufficiently gifted for the task of interpreting art; moreover the isolating of art, esthetics, the beautiful, and dwelling upon them exclusively, appeared to me as a kind of sickening, unhealthful perversion and onesidedness, devoid of roots in real soil" ("Some Biographical Remarks," 254).

Death) playing its own symphony with the fullest possible orchestration."[11] When he returned from the war, he wrote,

> I knew that I knew nothing whatsoever of things Indian, and that, even in
> the period when I took my Ph.D., I had not known anything real. . . . I
> said repeatedly to myself: I feel that now the time has come when some-
> one might understand something real of this Indian stuff [i.e. material,
> Ger. "Stoff"], if he had an archimedic point of support outside on which
> to base his other leg. This point, I felt, was to be gotten, not by books,
> research and libraries, but by living.[12]

He began to appreciate more fully the life around him in Germany:
"experiences with men and women, the magic scenery of Heidelberg
and the Neckar valley, and the discovery of non-Indic values in literature, art, music, psychology, medicine, helped me to come into my
own."[13] As Kenneth Zysk's paper explains, Zimmer began to supple-
ment the esoteric texts he had been studying with the more practical
material world of Indian medicine as he realized that he wished to
know more of ordinary life in India.

In 1932 Zimmer met C. G. Jung, and the meeting marked a water-
shed in Zimmer's life. Zimmer had already read *The Secret of the Golden
Flower*, a Chinese alchemical text, edited by Jung and Richard Wilhelm—and when they met he told Jung that he had been so infuriated
by Jung's psychological commentary that "he threw the book at the
wall." He also told Jung that upon further reading of the book, "What
struck me then was the sudden insight that my Sanskrit texts were
not simply a collection of grammatical and syntactical problems, but
that they also actually contained a substantial body of meaning." Jung
himself says that this bit of hyperbole should be taken with a grain
of salt; surely what Zimmer recognized was that Jung shared this
appreciation.[14]

This hyperbole is, however, an indication of the enthusiasm with
which Zimmer looked to Jung as a friend and guide. In Jung, Zimmer
found someone with whom he felt he had a close intellectual and spiritual kinship. Zimmer always thirsted for companions who were good
listeners—he lived by talk—and

> you cannot just talk to the stars or to the silence of the night. You have to
> fancy some listener, or, better yet, to know of somebody whose mere exis-

---

[11] "Some Biographical Remarks," 250.

[12] Ibid., 253.

[13] Ibid., 253–54.

[14] Reminiscences recorded by Aniela Jaffé, printed in *Erinnerungen Träume Gedanken
von C. G. Jung*, edited by Aniela Jaffé (Zurich: Rascher, 1962), 385–86, and translated in
the preface to *Artistic Form and Yoga*, xx.

tence stimulates you to talk and lends wings to your thoughts. In this respect the mere existence of Jung, quite apart from what I got out of meeting him, the mere fact that nature allowed this unique, mountainous example of the human species to come into existence, was, and is, one of the major blessings of my spiritual and my very earthly life.[15]

The talk Zimmer gave to the Analytical Psychology Club of New York in 1942, reprinted in this volume, shows how willing Zimmer was to cast Jung in the role of teacher, a "Zen master." He spoke of Jung as a teacher "the kind of which I had never encountered before in the flesh, and had never expected to meet alive in times like ours, but which was very familiar to me from Hindu tales and dialogues of sages, yogins, wizards and gurus."[16]

Jung, on his part, was quite willing to assume this role. He, too, knew of Zimmer before they met, having read "his fascinating book *Kunstform und Yoga* and long wished to meet him in person. I found him to be a man of lively temperament, a man of genius. He talked a great deal and spoke very rapidly, but he could also be an excellent, attentive listener. We spent several fine days together in wide-ranging conversations that for me at least proved extraordinarily situmu- lating."[17] But there is no doubt—in the written record, at least—which one played the role of student, and which was the teacher.

Jung acknowledged acquiring information about India from Zim- mer; on his side, Zimmer learned a whole new framework of think- ing, which seemed to provide an opening in European thought and culture for the kind of insights he was pursuing in the Indian mate- rial. But at about the same time, there appears to have been a subtle shift in Zimmer's enthusiastic acceptance of this material. Up to this time Zimmer wholeheartedly accepted the feeling that India was unknown territory worth exploring because there were truths to be found there.

> I had faith. Not the faith ever to understand or to decipher the charac- ters of the strange other script. But the faith that they contained as much truth, no more and no less, than the familiar script in which I was brought

[15] "Some Biographical Remarks," 260.

[16] Ibid. Jung was not the first older man Zimmer was to adopt as a teacher on an Asian model. Joseph Campbell wrote in an obituary of Zimmer that it was "the distinguished Dutch Sinologist Johann Maria de Groot—'a perfect embodiment,' as Zimmer described him, 'of the gentle wise Taoist Old Man'—who awakened his interest in Tantric Bud- dhism." See Campbell, "Heinrich Zimmer (1890–1943)," *Partisan Review* 20, no. 4 (July– August 1953): 447.

[17] *Erinnerungen Träume Gedanken von C. G. Jung,* translated in the preface to *Artistic Form and Yoga,* xix.

up and which was taken for the script of knowledge and reality all around me.[18]

Before meeting Jung, Zimmer's exuberant exploration of this material and the affirmation of the truth of its insights dominated his writing. After Zimmer met Jung, however, his writing became more cautious, as if some doubts had finally found a voice. The early years of their friendship coincided with the increasingly difficult times in Nazi Germany, and it was as if Jung had given him the language to express at least indirectly the discouragement that he must have felt even as he continued to exude good-humored vitality.

Zimmer was always aware that he could not simply and romantically adopt Indian teachings as a refuge in his own troubles. "We are not free to appropriate the great symbols of other times and places as our own," he said in 1933,

and speak of ourselves directly through them. They are a picture writing that summons us to [grasp] a reality that has always [existed], in ourselves as in the men of the past, and to live [from] it in new images and concepts, if the picture writing of our own tradition has either become meaningless to us, or as metaphoric as that of [all] vanishing historical eras.[19]

In this dark age, then, we cannot grasp the "great symbols" that have lived in other places, other times. We must accept what is available to us: "depth psychology," which transforms cosmology into psychology.

If we cannot raise our spiritual eye and find our regent in the heavens, we can discern it in inward voices and signs, as [happened to] Socrates; and, after all, is its situation in space anything more than imagery, a metaphoric visualization? What is the deeper relation of outward to inward, of macrocosm to microcosm? The merit of the new depth psychology is that it unearths that which is timeless in us, in a form appropriate to our time, so that we can comprehend it and live by it. This psychology and the analytic method by which it operates . . . is a science born of our time and our predicament with which it will also pass away, but for that very reason it is to us more intelligible than any other set of symbols; precisely because it is the only form in which we can validly explain to ourselves how we live, it puts us into relation with the very same reality which

[18] "Some Biographical Remarks," 249.
[19] "On the Significance of the Indian Tantric Yoga," in *Spiritual Disciplines: Papers from the Eranos Yearbooks*, Bollingen Series XXX.4 (New York: Pantheon, 1960), 28. Translation corrected by Gerald Chapple.

speaks through the fading hieroglyphic systems of other ages.... A meaningful doctrine can never be anything other than an arrow aimed at reality, the intangible reality which transcends the sphere of the intellect and of speech. The arrow, however, can graze this sphere, and our comprehension follows. Every age has different arrows; some ages have but a single arrow.[20]

He brought this sense of limitations into his understanding of India itself, that metaphor for his own consciousness:

The ritual path of the Hindu is bordered with sacraments, framed by customs, festivals, observances, as a highway is bordered by trees. In their shade he lives; they seize hold of him before he is born and they have power to find him long after his death. These observances stand side by side with the myths related in epics and countless old traditions, which guide men through life and create a bond between them by providing them with symbols and formulas for the reality of the world and of human destiny. The moral element in the myths, the example and warning, is concentrated in these observances. In their psychagogic function such observances are related to Yoga, and their specific character throws light upon the specific character of Yoga.[21]

Spiritual discipline is not now a path into the unknown, but a guided tour of a bounded world. Man is not an active agent, but the plaything of powerful forces. His goal is not to free himself from his bondage, but to get along with his fellow captives. Zimmer's enthusiastic empathy has changed into analytical observation and description, and in the process the conviction that what he writes of has a truth that we can hope to share—and should hope to share—has been lost. This sense of limitation is perhaps clearest when Zimmer describes the process by which the student of yoga internalizes his vision of the deity: "piece by piece, the entire image is inwardly evoked and enduringly held fast. The god's neck and arms, breast and flanks, are adorned with 'spiritual,' i.e., purely visualized ornaments, from the diadem in his hair to the bracelets round his ankles; 'spiritual' flowers are presented to him."[22] When Zimmer wrote *Kunstform und Yoga*, the word "spiritual" would never have been in quotation marks. Zimmer's imaginative re-creation of India is now more thoroughly filtered through his analytical intelligence—the very faculty he had found so limiting as a student.

C. G. Jung's understanding of India is interesting in this context; it points to how he seems to have put a damper on Zimmer's embrace of that culture. In 1938, shortly before Zimmer had to leave Germany,

[20] Ibid., 28–29.
[21] Ibid., 3.
[22] Ibid., 12–13.

Jung made a trip to India. Jung recalled later that Zimmer "had been interested for years in the Maharshi of Tiruvannamalai, and the first question he asked me on my return from India concerned this latest holy and wise man from southern India." In Shri Ramana Maharshi, said Jung, Zimmer saw "the true avatar of the figure of the *rishi*, seer and philosopher, which strides, as legendary as it is historical, down the centuries and the ages"—the place Jung himself filled in Zimmer's European life.[23] Jung found himself unable—unwilling—to visit this man his friend so admired. "I simply could not, despite the uniqueness of the occasion, bring myself to visit this undoubtedly distinguished man personally." Why? Jung's immediate explanation was disingenuous. "For the fact is," he continued,

> I doubt his uniqueness; he is of a type that always was and will be. Therefore it was not necessary to seek him out. I saw him all over India. . . . He is "genuine," and on top of that he is a "phenomenon" which, seen through European eyes, has claims to uniqueness. But in India he is merely the whitest spot on a white surface.

With one stroke, Jung wiped out the endless variation, the extremes that are to be found in every aspect of India. He went on immediately to exclaim, "Altogether, one sees so much in India that in the end one only wishes one could see less."[24]

Jung came with a picture of the "real" India that his experience during his short visit confirmed. This India, as Mary Linda's paper makes clear, closely parallels Hegel's; it is ethereal, a dream world. "Shri Ramana's thoughts," Zimmer wrote, "are beautiful to read. What one finds here is purest India, the breath of eternity, scorning and scorned by the world."[25] It follows, of course, that what is true for India and Indians is unique and not shared by the European:

> There is no village or country road where that broad-branched tree cannot be found in whose shade the ego struggles for its own abolition, drowning the world of multiplicity in the All and All-Oneness of Universal Being. This note rang so insistently in my ears that soon I was no longer able to shake off its spell. I was then absolutely certain that no one could ever get beyond this, least of all the Indian holy man himself; and should Shri Ramana say anything that did not chime in with this melody,

[23] C. G. Jung, "Introduction" to Heinrich Zimmer, *Der Weg zum Selbst: Lehre und Leben des indischen Heiligen Shri Ramana Maharshi aus Tiruvannamalai* (Zurich, 1944), translated by R.F.C. Hull as "The Holy Men of India" in *Psychology and Religion: West and East*, vol. 11 of *The Collected Works of C. G. Jung*, Bollingen Series XX, 2d ed. (Princeton: Princeton University Press, 1969), 576, 581. Zimmer's last work before his death was this translation of some of Shri Ramana Maharshi's English-language writings into German.

[24] Ibid., 577.

[25] Ibid., 579.

or claim to know anything that transcended it, his illumination would assuredly be false. The holy man is right when he intones India's ancient chants, but wrong when he pipes any other tune. This effortless drone of argumentation, so suited to the heat of southern India, made me refrain, without regret, from a visit to Tiruvannamalai.[26]

And yet, if he could learn nothing from the great teacher, Jung felt that he had learned something from one of his followers. "The unfathomableness of India," he said,

saw to it that I should encounter the holy man after all, in a form that was more congenial to me.... I ran across a disciple of the Maharshi. He was an unassuming little man ... [with] innumerable children to feed.... I acknowledge with deep gratitude this meeting with him; nothing better could have happened to me.

This man had the reality of daily life about him:

My man—thank God—was only a little holy man; no radiant peak above the dark abysses, no shattering sport of nature, but an example of how wisdom, holiness, and humanity can dwell together in harmony, richly, pleasantly, sweetly, and patiently, without limiting one another, without being peculiar, causing no surprise, in no way sensational, necessitating no special post-office, yet embodying an age-old culture amid the gentle murmur of the coconut palms fanning themselves in the light sea wind.[27]

Unthreatened by any mountainous beings on a farther shore, Jung returned to Europe; one wonders how he explained his trip to Zimmer. "I do not know whether my friend found it an unforgivable or an incomprehensible sin on my part that I had not sought out Shri Ramana," he recalled.[28]

[26] Ibid., 578.

[27] Ibid., 578–79.

[28] Ibid., 576. In 1947 Joseph Campbell reviewed *Der Weg zum Selbst* in *Review of Religion* 11, no. 3 (March 1947): 290–93. He first commented on the greatness of Zimmer as a translator of this "unsurpassed interpreter" of India's traditional wisdom, quoting among other things one of Shri Ramana's teachings: "The bliss of pure Self can unfold only to an Imagination that has been clarified and made steady, as the result of constantly practiced meditation. He who has experienced in himself this bliss, is 'Redeemed in this life'" (a quotation that sheds light on Campbell's famous phrase "follow your bliss"). Campbell then comments, "The introduction supplied by Dr. Jung, on the other hand, is concerned to devaluate both the metaphysical tradition of India and the personality of the present teacher, and to represent the superiority of Dr. Jung's own definition of the Self. This is done by slightly misrepresenting the teaching of the Maharshi.... Dr. Jung has made it a little too easy for himself and his Western readers (for whom the metaphysical is an outmoded form of experience and discussion) to assume the superior part." I am grateful to Gerald Chapple for pointing me to this review.

One also wonders what Zimmer's own reaction to India would have been if he had been able to travel there. Would he have found India itself unpleasant, like Jung and Mircea Eliade and many others who have loved Indian myths? I suspect not. As his widow wrote, he could accept so much. It is hard to imagine that he would turn away from India as he found it.

As it was, he traveled to America, not India. The idea in Zimmer's works that myths and dreams are variations of the same phenomenon, which also inspired Jung, involved the two of them in a sympathetic circle of friends on both sides of the Atlantic. Zimmer escaped Germany in 1939 and, after a brief stay in Oxford, arrived in the United States in 1940. William McGuire's paper explores his place in the circle around Paul and Mary Mellon and the Bollingen Foundation they sponsored, and how he drew the young Joseph Campbell into this circle—a connection that was to make Zimmer's name known, posthumously, to a wide audience, and that provided Campbell a springboard for his brilliant career.

This volume opens with two recollections of Zimmer, one by his daughter Maya Rauch, the other by a close friend and supporter in Germany, Herbert Nette. Then William McGuire describes Zimmer's connections with Mary and Paul Mellon and with the Jungian circles in Switzerland and New York. A brief talk by Zimmer, previously unpublished, describes his admiration of C. G. Jung. Wendy Doniger picks up the question of Zimmer's intellectual legacy, especially in the light of Joseph Campbell's editorial work on his English publications. Gerald Chapple raises another question about how his influence was felt: the division between what is known of his work in the German- and the English-speaking worlds. Kenneth Zysk then summarizes and analyzes Zimmer's contribution to Western knowledge of Hindu medicine; Matthew Kapstein evaluates his place in the West's appreciation of Indian philosophy; and Mary Linda discusses his contributions to the study of Indian art in the light of A. K. Coomaraswamy's work and more recent research.

All the papers in this volume testify to Zimmer's originality and to his rightful place in that small group of great scholars—which includes A. K. Coomaraswamy and Stella Kramrisch—who were part of the first generation to confront the end of European empires in India and the rest of Asia. They were among the first to try to decolonize the European mind. Their insights can still fertilize our thought.

1

HEINRICH ZIMMER FROM A

DAUGHTER'S PERSPECTIVE

Maya Rauch

I LAST SAW my father when I was fourteen years old, in 1939. He had to leave Germany with his wife and three sons, and I had to stay with my mother and two brothers. I was part of his "other family," which I should explain, since it sheds light on his life and work.

In 1923 Heinrich Zimmer met and fell in love with Mila Esslinger-Rauch (1886–1972). He considered the relationship the beginning of his "coming into his own," and he regarded his first book, *Kunstform und Yoga im indischen Kultbild* (1926), as a fruit of the love they shared. Mila was an Austrian, married to Eugen Esslinger (1870–1944), a German Jew sixteen years older than her. He had discovered her talent as a painter and had allowed her to study art in Paris and the Netherlands before the First World War. He was a bit like a father to her and accepted her relationship with Zimmer, never wanting a divorce. Esslinger gave Mila's three children by Zimmer (Maya, b. 1925; Ernst Michael, 1926–1945; Lukas, b. 1932) his own name. Zimmer, on his part, had a very small salary as Privatdozent at Heidelberg University and did not feel able to marry Mila.

Esslinger had inherited enough money to live comfortably until the inflation around 1925, when he lost his entire fortune. In 1927 he went with Mila and her first two children to America, where he had obtained a job as a librarian at the University of Michigan in Ann Arbor. Meanwhile, Zimmer and Christiane von Hofmannsthal decided to marry. In the spring of 1928 he told Christiane that there was another woman he loved, who was in America with their two children and with whom he would never break up his relationship. Christiane was willing to go along with the relationship—America was at that time rather far away.

But Mila Esslinger was very unhappy in her exile and came back to Germany in the fall of 1928; Eugen Esslinger returned some time later. Until his emigration in 1939, Heinrich Zimmer shared his life between the two women he loved. Christiane and Mila never met, but they accepted each other; there was no quarrel between them.

Heinrich Zimmer had to leave Germany in 1939, with his half-Jewish wife, Christiane. Before he left, he declared himself the father of Mila's children and told the German authorities that he wanted them to have his name. In 1941 the children received a "proof of Aryan descent" from the government and the maiden name of their mother, Rauch.

Looking at my father now—being myself older than he ever became—I am again and again impressed by his productivity and his capacity for work. Apart from his duties at Heidelberg University, he would lecture at other places, such as the C. G. Jung Club in Zurich and in Basel or the Eranos meetings in Ascona. In addition to his main publications, such as *Kunstform und Yoga* and *Maya*, he contributed to magazines and newspapers and wrote reviews, as well as translating with his wife Christiane the almost endless *History of India* by Sir George Dunbar. Moreover, in 1929, after the sudden death of his father-in-law, Hugo von Hofmannsthal, he became responsible for the posthumous edition of the latter's works, although he refused to be named the editor. With the help of Christiane, who had at times been her father's secretary, he took charge of the literary estate of Hofmannsthal, producing two volumes of shorter texts, one of poems, and the novel *Andreas*, for which, as in many other cases, he had to fit unconnected fragments together.

He also started a collection of Hofmannsthal's letters, editing two volumes in the period from 1935 to 1937, and sending a third to the publisher in the spring of 1940, when he was in Oxford. A wide-ranging correspondence documents his struggles to gather the texts and to get his mother-in-law's permission to publish them. In the beginning she was afraid that her late husband might not have wanted them published. He had to convince her and some of her advisors, old friends of Hofmannsthal; in the case of the poems he also had to convince the publisher, who for other reasons did not want to see the entire collection appear. This was the toughest battle—and on two fronts—he ever had to fight, writing letters speaking "the language of man and even of angels" until he was able to have all but two of the poems published. He had no secretary to type his manuscripts and letters or to read the proofs, except on rare occasions—as in the case of the Hofmannsthal publications—when others such as Dr. Herbert Steiner helped him.

From 1933 on, the terrible circumstances in Germany caused by the Third Reich made the lives of many of his friends and of his own family difficult, even unbearable. In the winter of 1937–1938 he was dismissed from the University of Heidelberg and lost his professorial title. Finding no adequate position, and having hardly any income, he had to leave the country. When he emigrated in 1939, first to England and then in 1940 to America, he was dependent on the generous help of others. Even his lectures in the first years at Columbia University were paid for by members of the C. J. Jung Club, his "Mahatmas from Manhattan," until he was finally taken onto the payroll of the university in the winter of 1942–1943, some months before his sudden death.

But as I remember him from a child's perspective, he was always in good spirits, always seemed to have time, never complained about life or about having too much work. In Heidelberg he would come to the family breakfast having already returned from the post office, where he had mailed the letters he had written earlier in the morning—for he liked to get up early—and he rejoiced in having gotten on with his own work; he was often enthusiastic about some new idea that had just struck him. He could be impatient when we interrupted him while he was working or speaking to other people, or when we were too noisy or behaved in a silly way, but the rest of the time he was good humored, took part in our activities, encouraged us in things we were doing, such as drawing pictures based on stories we had read.

When he was away on journeys, he sent us postcards of works of art he had seen, always with a short comment on the back: "This is Christ appearing to Maria Magdalena as a gardener after his resurrection" (by Fra Angelico of S. Marco in Florence), or "This, to say the least, is what hell looks like!" (So sieht die Hölle aus, mindestens)—writing about the picture of hell in Campo Santo at Pisa. When later in life I visited an art gallery, it was always like coming home, meeting the familiar paintings that I had once collected.

He went out with us on long walks, taking us by our hands—his hands I remember always being warm—and speaking with us about things that were important to us at the time, telling us stories of his own youth, or others like "Abu Kasem's Slippers" or "The King and the Corpse." At home he would read us fairy tales and myths he was dealing with, and when some inspiration had come to him while he was reading, he would write a note on a scrap of paper, as he always had some paper in his pocket. He also read Shakespeare—I remember *Macbeth*; novels—mostly of German romanticism; poetry, especially ballads; and of course he read the Bible to us.

I remember my father reading about the conquest of Jericho from a children's Bible with pictures when I was about five. Later, when I was eight or nine years old, he would read to us from the voluminous Luther Bible—at least all the narrative parts of it. I still hear Abraham

bargaining with the Lord about the number of innocent people necessary to spare Sodom, starting with fifty and gradually getting down to
ten. He read the passage with real delight, adopting the manner of an
old Eastern Jew. He was fond of the Jewish world. When we read Exo-
dus, I was impressed by the help the Israelites received from the Lord
in escaping from Egypt, how they were guided by the pillar of cloud,
which was fire at night, how they were led through the Red Sea while
the pursuers were destroyed, and how they went on through the desert, the Lord giving them all they needed: water, manna, and quail.
And yet the Israelites, His Chosen People, again and again complained
to Moses, wishing to be back in Egypt in slavery, and recalling the
abundance of food there. Then, just when Miriam was punished for
her disobedience and the rebellious Korah and his followers were
swallowed by the earth, I said to my father, "I can't understand why
they are so disobedient and not very grateful, when the Lord is caring
for them so especially." And he answered, "Well, you must realize
what it meant for them to plod through the desert, stop whenever the
pillar of cloud halted above the Ark of the Covenant, unpack their be-
longings, put up their tents—and when they had just settled down, the
pillar of cloud would move on, and they had to get up and pack their
things together and move on . . . and you know, even manna becomes
tedious in time."

My father looked on mythology and religious tradition with deep
awe and realism at the same time. I believe that one reason for his
productivity was that life and learning for him were never separated.
All his work was part of his life and his life part of his work. The answers he found in dealing with religion were valid for himself, as some
of his letters show. And he shared this attitude with us children, treat-
ing us as equal partners in the discussion. I was about nine years old
when, as I came home from school, he asked me what we were learning just then. It was "the cyclical process of water." I had to explain to
him how it worked: the rain comes down from the clouds, is absorbed
by the earth, then appears again in a well, becomes a stream, and turns
into a river flowing into the sea, where the water evaporates and become clouds again; and the cycle can begin anew. And he added,
"Well, all nature is part of this cycle, all plants, all creatures, and you
yourself, your blood, your sweat is part of it." While he spoke he
raised his arm, and I remember some sweat on it—it was summer. The
cyclical process had just acquired another dimension for me, and I
gained a feeling of being part of creation in quite a realistic way.

He felt at home in nature. You must remember that nature at that
time did not yet seem in danger; air, water, and earth were not pol-
luted, and the lovely landscape around Heidelberg still looked as it

had looked for centuries. There was a railway, but neither modern industries nor modern highways had altered the land. Destruction began only in the late thirties, when Hitler began to build the Autobahn and modern traffic developed, together with industrialization. My father was fond of walking through the country or riding his bicycle. He loved swimming in the Neckar River, which was in its upper parts still free of weirs and was rather wild, and he enjoyed going out in the garden in a summer thunderstorm, when rain and hail were pouring down. He would go out just in shorts, feeling the rain on his bare skin. Meals often were like a feast in his company. He liked to drink wine, especially in the evening. He was fond of life, and perhaps it was for this very reason that he never clung to it. He was also fully aware of all the misery and hardship creatures have to go through. There was some melancholy deep in him, especially in his later years, which could be felt at moments. But he never complained. As Christiane wrote after his death, "He could accept so much."

My father was a true and valuable friend, and he enjoyed the presence of his many friends, encouraging and helping them when he was able to. But here also his realism was at work: he saw their shortcomings and miseries, and as he liked to find appropriate expressions for everything, he would find witty words for these, too. His sense of humor and fun was almost always present; his letters are delightful to read. And he took the same attitude toward himself.

His friends in Heidelberg sometimes asked one another, "Who is able to stop Zimmer talking?" Very few could. When he was asked about or told something he was interested in, he would start a flowing monologue on the subject, forgetting that others might also like to say something. In fact, he was speaking until the very last moment of his life. When he was in the hospital dying of pneumonia, suffering from a high fever, he continued to speak about the books he was going to write, quoting Latin and Greek authors, naming historical persons. The nearer he came to death, though, the more he fell into pathos. Speaking was for my father a vehicle to gain knowledge. A good listener was a source of inspiration. Most of his thoughts he developed through speaking—"Ich errede mir alles." But he was well aware of his volubility and could joke about it.

And then there was his grief about failing to get to India. Ever since he had started reading Sanskrit, he had longed to go there, and this lifelong wish was never fulfilled. He tried three times, as far as I know. In those days it was much more expensive to get there than it is now, and he never had much money to spend in his life. The first time he tried was in the twenties; the company with which he had booked his journey and which he had paid for his ticket went bankrupt. He made a second attempt in 1935, when he was to lead a group of interested people through India. The plan failed because the German government considered him unsuitable for the task because he had a half-Jewish wife and refused him permission to go.

The last time he planned the trip was in 1939, when he was in England. But then the Second World War broke out. This time he had already bought the equipment—especially a sun helmet, which he carried to America. He later had a photograph made of himself wearing it on Cape Cod. He sent it to my mother, writing, "You see, the helmet is quite useful to me in the sun here at the Atlantic coast, and like Tartarin of Tarascon [the French bourgeois who boasted of lion-hunting in Algeria before he had ever been there] I can say, 'the helmet was with me in the jungles of India when I stood on one leg, my arms stretched to heaven and saying nothing, nothing, nothing' [und schweig und schweig und schweig]."

In order to appreciate this joke fully, one should remember that my father never tried the practice of yoga himself, and he was dubious about the Buddhist communities and monasteries that came into fashion in Germany during his time. He did not consider it sensible for us in the West to take over the forms of Indian religion, for we have such different traditions. At the same time, all his life was devoted to understanding other religions, with the attitude contained in the message given to the rabbi from Cracow by the officer on the bridge in Prague: that the treasure he had traveled such a long way to find was actually hidden in his own house. But the officer, who had dreamt of the same treasure as the rabbi, was not fully aware of what he was saying.

2

AN EPITAPH FOR HEINRICH ZIMMER

(1948)

Herbert Nette

(TRANSLATED BY JAMES B. LAWSON
AND GERALD CHAPPLE)

LET ME BEGIN my reminiscences of Heinrich Zimmer and his works with a few biographical notes. He was born on December 6, 1890, in Greifswald, the son of the scholar of Indian studies who bore the same name and to whom we are indebted for a definitive portrayal of Vedic culture. The younger Zimmer studied German and comparative philology in Berlin, presenting himself for *Habilitation* at the university in Greifswald soon after the end of World War I. From 1924 to 1938 he held the chair of Indian philology in Heidelberg, but lost his post there because he was married to Christiane von Hofmannsthal.[1] They emigrated with their children, first to Oxford, where he had been invited by the English government to give a series of lectures, and then, during the second year of the war, to America. It was in the United States that he died, on March 18, 1943, after a brief illness.[2]

In light of these few facts one might think it more appropriate that a professional philologist write an evaluation of a colleague's works. But such an assumption would fail to take into account the breadth and significance of the contributions of a scholar who refused to con-

Herbert Nette was a particularly helpful friend of Heinrich Zimmer's in the 1930s, who published his newspaper articles in the *Frankfurter Rundschau* after the Nazis had forbidden him to appear in print professionally. Nette's eulogy first appeared in *Merkur* 2, no. 3 (1948): 436–41; the version followed here is from the reprint in Herbert Nette, *Varia aus vier Jahrzehnten* (Darmstadt: Gesellschaft Hessischer Literaturfreunde, 1975), 58–66. Our thanks to Maya Rauch for supplying this document.—TRANS.

[1] The term *chair* is not accurate. Zimmer was *außerordentlicher Professor*, a rank roughly equivalent to that of a full professor but below that of *Ordinarius*, or chair-holder, in the German academic hierarchy. Christiane von Hofmannsthal was part Jewish.

[2] This should read March 20. Communication difficulties resulting from the war undoubtedly account for the fact that the date given in German sources for Zimmer's death is very often wrong.—TRANS.

fine himself within a narrow discipline. The territory he carved out as his creative, intellectual home was a triangle whose sides were the fields of art, science, and philosophy. That triangle became his home ground. I shall attempt to portray what brought him to make that choice and to show how profoundly Europe has benefited, and is still benefiting, from the riches he brought us from the treasure trove of the mythic age of India.

The title of one of his first books, *Ewiges Indien* [Eternal India (1930)], can be viewed as an epigraph for all the works that followed; his was an ongoing and valiant struggle not only to comprehend and articulate what is valid and vital for the Indian tradition but to show as well how that tradition is meaningful for the West. Although it is true that his studies, in their aims and methods, are different from the run-of-the-mill scholarship of Sanskrit specialists, they have nothing at all in common with attempts by certain others to adopt and adapt this alien world for the West by means of unrestrained empathizing or by trying to make it, in some superficial way, seem contemporary.

A prime example of Zimmer's work is his *Kunstform und Yoga im indischen Kultbild* [Artistic Form and Yoga in the Sacred Images of India (1926)]. The theosophists and aesthetes of the 1920s had affected a pose of patronizing familiarity when they attempted to explain, psychologically and "esoterically," icons that came from a religious sensibility foreign to us, from an artistic tradition completely other than our own. In none of Zimmer's work is there so much as a trace of that condescension. It was precisely the personal intensity with which Zimmer submerged himself in the total otherness and foreignness of the art object that made him doubt even the possibility of subjective empathy, not to mention the validity of conclusions based on it. He suspected that the West's methods of observation were totally inadequate for any attempt at comprehending the Buddhas or the sacred images of the gods and saints of the East; perception of their essence lay on a completely different plane that was accessible only to those familiar with their religious and cultic basis.

One of the most richly informative—and most beautiful—books about India ever written, his was the first to provide a key to understanding the real significance of the art of India's sacred images; until its publication, they had been neither understandable nor understood. Zimmer built his interpretations on the arcane traditions of medieval Hindu sects that the studies of the English scholar Sir Arthur Avalon had made accessible. Briefly summarized: the unique nature of the Indian sacred image, its fundamental difference from classical works of art, resides in the fact that both its sense and its purpose are totally contained in its function as a psychic tool for ritual worship. Zimmer discovered, furthermore, that no difference in essence or function exists between, on the one hand, the images of the saints or divinities and, on the other, their geometric symbolic counterparts, themselves imbued with the same cosmic and symbolic significance. In the eyes of the devout Indian initiate, they are identical; in fact, the geometric construct is often given preference over figural forms. Zimmer's identification of these various forms as a single ritual tool, a *yantra*, reveals how perverse any comparison with works of European art really is. A critical interpretation of those linear, geometric constructs as ornaments must remain just as futile as would pointless and nonsensical comment on the aesthetic qualities of the figural sacred images of India.

If it is true that our eyes, schooled as they are in classical tradition, are drawn or repelled by the Indian images by nothing more significant than subjective taste or chance, then the inadequacy of our vision becomes clear: our vision is simply incapable of penetrating to the mystery that lies at their heart and core. The most an noninitiate can ever perceive in the *yantra* is the image itself or some component part of that image; only the initiate or the adept in possession of suprasensual vision can perceive in this mundane apparatus the divine energy itself. Its essential being is not in any given image, nor does it, during the act of worship, enter the image from without. It is the worshiper, producing within himself a vision of divine reality, who projects that vision into the image before him. For the Indian, the goal of worship of the divine is to become oneself divine.

Once the real nature of the sacred image is understood, it becomes evident that our European ways of seeing, our methods of aesthetic criticism, cannot begin to understand those forms even superficially. A work of classical art (Zimmer always means this in the broadest sense) is made for the eye to behold and exists for the sole purpose of being seen by a discriminating eye. "Our eye is expected to scan every part of the work—it is on parade before us. But Indian sculpture is in repose, sufficient unto itself."[3] The whole of Western art is the reproduction of the phenomenal world and, when most successful, an expression of an object's inner essence. Indian *yantras*, by contrast, are "simply a means of mirroring eternal essence ensnared in the illusory world, and ... represent Truth only to someone who does not yet know what Truth is."[4] The inherent contrasts outlined here help explain the contempt, even the revulsion, with which Goethe, himself totally in thrall to the classical tradition, rejected what he called the "grotesque nature" of Indian sculpture. A work of classical art is

[3] Heinrich Zimmer, *Artistic Form and Yoga in the Sacred Images of India*, trans. Gerald Chapple and James B. Lawson in collaboration with J. Michael McKnight (Princeton: Princeton University Press, 1984), 13–14.—TRANS.
[4] Ibid., 227.—TRANS.

always "beautiful" to the extent that it celebrates phenomenal reality, apparent reality, and to the degree that it records the enchantment of existence, unfolding the veil of *maya* and glorifying it. But the most exhalted aim and purpose of classical art, that which absorbs its total energy, is totally peripheral and incidental to a *yantra*. "Essence" lies behind and beyond the veil the sacred image represents, which in itself may well be in our eyes a thing of beauty, since the divine frequently manifests itself in forms that are beautiful. It is there that "essence" lies, revealing itself to the adept only when he is concentrated in his suprasensual vision; it is there where lies the "inmost core" "before which words and even thought itself must retreat without ever having reached it."[5]

With this, his first book, Zimmer put an end to an era that had been content to produce purely aesthetic judgments on Indian art, or simple iconographic descriptions. In his subsequent works, he spread Indian legends of the gods and creation myths so enticingly before our eyes that we can now begin to divine the meaning of the hieroglyphics of the irrational contained in their exotic names and figures, in their gestures and their worlds.

At this point, one is tempted to ask if anything meaningful for our own reality can be drawn from the cosmos of Indian myth. If one looks upon myth as no more than the outward expression of some archaic level of consciousness, the answer must be no; such a stage, distinct as it is from any rational process of thought, could rouse only as much interest as might be afforded anything else that has survived from times long gone. However, there has been a growing awareness since the pioneering work of Schelling and Bachofen, and increasingly since the turn of the century, that myth, in its patterns and images, is the repository of a timeless power to envision and to interpret life through figures and images. Only after myth is accepted on its own terms and comprehended as a timeless way of relating to the world, only when the mythic heart of our own being is stirred, do we really begin to start experiencing its meaning.

What this method achieves is more compelling than what mere comparative mythology sets out to do and actually does; likewise, Zimmer's enterprise is just as far removed from the numerous forms of gnosticism and occult magic that flourished in the 1920s. One of the salient characteristics in the psychological makeup of that time was its susceptibility to the spirit of the East (or what, after superficial contact with a few writings of dubious provenance, was then understood to be that spirit). But as far as any real approximation to Eastern models is concerned, all those programs of eclectic theosophy, or of occult train-

[5] Ibid., 232.—TRANS.

ing exercises, never amounted to anything more than a questionable attempt to connect widely opposing points of view by some kind of spiritual short circuit, whether their starting point was suprasensual perception, the control of supposed physiological centers, or the "salvation of the self," attained by means of gymnastic or hygienic exercises. If the West has anything at all worth setting beside the extraordinary perceptions deriving from Indian introversion, it is something of a totally different nature: the system of depth psychology propounded by C. G. Jung. Zimmer was always aware of the tension between the heterogenous states of consciousness peculiar to myth and to psychoanalysis, respectively; this opened up the possibility of a breakthrough to a stratum of human experience common to them both, one that at a subterranean level joins East and West, two worlds apparently so distant from each other and even occasionally antogonistic toward each other. Zimmer's preeminent concern was the human being as a historical and contemporaneous entity.

His most important work is still the comprehensive volume entitled *Maya: Der indische Mythos* [Maya: The Myths of India (1963)]. His enormous power of language enabled him to transpose the artistic subtleties of a highly stylized hymnic and epic language so expertly that we succumb completely to the marvel of it all, to the atmosphere of Indian legend: its nebulous antiquity, its wealth of portent, its baroque confusion, its tropical welter of forms and shapes, its dreamlike mergings, its operatic colorfulness and shimmering aura. In this respect, his work deserves a place beside other great translations of world literature into German, translations of such quality that they have become part of the national literature itself. It is surely more than mere chance that his home in those years was Heidelberg, the chief center of German romanticism. It was Heidelberg that had provided the right intellectual and spiritual atmosphere for Schlegel, Brentano, and Creuzer; and now again, in the case of Zimmer, the *genius loci* proved as effective as in times past.

In characterizing the spirit that informs *Maya*, that junglelike tangle of fairy tales, one might well quote Hegel: "What we find represented here is God in the rapture of his dreaming." How often in our deepest dreams do familiar beings appear transformed, every dream figure a surrogate! This repeated emergence and submergence in the self was once dealt with in the language of this Indian myth:[6]

A saint goes forth to discover and understand God's *maya*, the form in which the divine conceals itself from the perception of its creations. The

[6] The following is Nette's abbreviating paraphrase of a myth Zimmer retells in *Maya: Der indische Mythos* (Stuttgart: Deutscher Verlags-Anstalt, 1936), 39–40.—TRANS.

God, aware of the saint's intent, bids him submerge himself in the sea. Having done so, the saint discovers he is a maiden, a princess, espoused to a king, is delivered of sons, blessed with grandchildren, enjoys a happy life and great power. Then her spouse and her father become enemies; in the great battle ensuing, both are slain. All her sons and grandsons perish. With loud lamenting she constructs the funeral pyre: "Alas! my sons!" she cries, and leaps into the flames, only to find herself once again in the sea, once again the saint. With a loud laugh the God addressed him, saying: "Where, O fool, are the sons for whom you mourn? Of such is the form of my *maya*. How can you ever hope to know the unfathomable!"

In this myth the experience of déjà vu ("I've experienced this once before, ages ago") finds a profound rationale, because here all of life appears as an interlinking of transformations. Is there anything more alien, or less acceptable, to us Westerners? Not just its atmosphere and exotic setting, its psychological form, but, more particularly, its implicit metaphysical point of view? This alarming house of mirrors; the ever-changing masks produced by the belief in the transmigration of souls; the perception of life as a deep, deep dream from which we must awake; and, finally, the ironic pose which, when all is over and done, attaches not the least bit of importance either to our own heroic struggles or to the agonies of the gods. Zimmer's aim, far from being an attempt to minimize the distance separating us from the East, is to expound, often with profound insight, on those very differences between Orient and Occident:

The Indian has simply never, even in his wildest dreams, conceived of a cosmic order whose final purpose and meaning could endure more than a moment, lasting longer than that twinkling of an eye; his cosmos is constantly in transition, always moving. Christianity's "Church Triumphant" is supposed ultimately to put a glorious end to all "strife" here below; the Indian finds an appropriate image in the rhythm of the Round Dance that never ends. The West, convinced as it is of the world's perfectability, finds itself totally disconcerted by the almost cosmic indifference of the Indian. But from the point of view of Indian myth, the unwillingness to make an attempt to grasp this infinite play of the circle is in essence diabolical.[7]

But all the differences separating East and West become trivial once we come to see myth as the articulating organ of the unconscious: this is the very understanding to which Zimmer's work is leading, or misleading, us. For it is in myth where, in defiance of all literary or even verbal categorization, an irrepressible vitality (which is precisely what

[7] Ibid., 140–41.—TRANS.

the psychological term *the unconscious* means) appears in an ever-changing round dance of masks and transformations, in a never-ending series of rebirths and transitions. In this boundless realm, in this fathomless sea, the Indian lives like an amphibian, not yet cast up upon the dry land of the Promethean realm of consciousness; he is no Western European, who is able only to proffer up the tiny blossom of conscious self, to raise it above the surface of the sea.

Zimmer had the knack of making his reader's contact with a subject rewarding. He never misused his talent by attempting a psychological interpretation of matters that were in themselves mysteries. His approach to the legends and myths of India was marked by a cautious reverence both toward the outward spiritual manifestations of an alien people and to the very essence of myth itself. He always kept in mind that any interpretation is merely one of several possibilities; that the interpreter must recognize when he must step back, being careful not to upstage the phenomenon whose nature he is attempting to explain. In spite of the wealth of Zimmer's searching, often profoundly penetrating insights, his commentaries are never stretched so far as to compromise, or even destroy, the integrity of the myth through excessive rationality. He once said of himself that he always took great pains to make sure "his own words did not blunt the razor-sharp points that, without anyone's help, are already capable of piercing through to the very heart of their mark."

Would it be appropriate here to offer personal details about a man whose life was devoted to the study of a universe that ignores the individual as an individual? A universe that recognizes the concept of person only in the sense of a disputed etymological derivation: *persona*, from *personare*, the word for the actor's mask through which his voice resounds? It is, I think, quite appropriate. For many of us who knew him, Heinrich Zimmer's person and conversation were even more fascinating than what he revealed of himself in his writings. A novelist, now deceased, once used the great scholar and psychologist of India as a model for one of his characters, giving us this description of the "mask" through which his voice was projected:[8]

> a rounded brow, prominent veins, the hair brushed back but not flattened, bushy, as if wind-blown—an imposing head that created its own nimbus! The eyebrows were shaggy, slanting downwards and to the side;

[8] Max Kommerell (1902–1944), a writer and professor of literature in Marburg, published *Der Lampenschirm aus den drei Taschentüchern* (Berlin: Fischer, 1941), a novel featuring Zimmer as "Professor Ferdinand Neander." Zimmer's humorous expression of thanks from the early summer of 1941 has been published in Maya Rauch and Dorothea Mussgenug, "Briefe aus dem Exil: Aus der Korrespondenz von Heinrich Zimmer, 1939–1943," *Heidelberger Jahrbücher* 35 (1991): 235–36.—TRANS.

the upper eyelids were very large, narrowing toward the outer corners; a deep-seated gleam was harbored within the paleness of eyes that were themselves not very large. As if to compensate for that hidden gleam, his mouth was profligate in the volume of its resonant sound; it was the mouth of an elemental force of nature. Seen in profile, the line between nose and mouth was extraordinarily long and slanted forward, making the upper lip protrude and lending the face a somewhat boyishly pugnacious air. The mouth itself was not clearly defined, just an opening, a gash—basically a means for channeling those torrents upon torrents of words. It was plain that we were in the presence of a demagogue who could stir men's minds; and above all: that huge, arching chest, the source from which sprang that powerful voice, incredibly massive, rising and falling conspicuously with each breath he drew.

Channeling those torrents of words . . . the joy he derived from talking, the sheer volume of his conversation was indeed extraordinary, a delight for everyone upon whom he showered it. He needed another living, breathing person to talk with. "I get all my ideas by talking," he used to say of himself. And how true it was: as he spoke, he managed to imbue everything with color and brilliance, with profound meaning. He could discover hidden significance in any object at all or in everyday occurrences. He saw the world as an entity, not compartmentalized into disciplines. He had only contempt for patchwork or for half-truths; he was always trying to see everything as a whole. Everything on earth was interconnected, if you just probed beneath the surface. He managed to compare some wretched sculpture on an ashtray he had dug up in Paris with a late Classical representation of Mithras, pointing out how and where the symbolism had gone underground when it became unacceptable to the conventional world. He could talk half the night long about Goethe's *Die Wahlverwandtschaften*, or about a poem by Hofmannsthal, a poet he idolized from his earliest youth; he could go on about the symbolism of playing cards, something he intended to write a book about—and perhaps even did, once he got to America. At times like these he seemed to be in a state of temporary exaltation, an impression that was heightened by the sharpness of his wit, by his penchant for making acid comments about mediocrities on the political scene, and by the sharpness of his dazzling wit.

But anyone close to him could not fail to notice the melancholy underlying all this élan. The sense of calm resignation that characterized his attitude toward the times is evident in these few words from his letter informing me of his dismissal from Heidelberg: "As an inveterate romantic, I am attracted to lost causes, anywhere, at any time. Marching ahead to the strains of triumphal marches à la Verdi really

1. Zimmer in New Rochelle, New York, 1941 or 1942.

isn't for the likes of me." By the same token he would have found it unthinkable to abandon the apparently lost cause of Western civilization or to forget the fate of the Old World as he adapted himself to the New. And it was there he died, after an illness lasting only a few days. When I heard it was pneumonia to which his body succumbed, I wondered about his frame of mind in those final days. One of the last letters to make its way to me across the ocean shows how thoroughly he had absorbed and taken to heart the teachings of the East. He had reached his own conclusions.

> People in our day and age have just come to the edge of the shore of the sea of tears and suffering they have yet to cross. . . . But only when you sense that everything that happens to you, and is somehow connected with you, is something that really belongs to you as a unified whole— only then can you understand your own fate and sense its meaning: that is *amor fati*. A fate we cannot transform into meaning will crush us. We must tear away the veil from the demon who approaches us, its face hidden, and must call it by name, exclaiming: "I know you, I know who you are—you are me!" We are ourselves the meaning that gives life; our breath, our vision, ourselves, and the very fact that we keep moving ahead create purpose and patterns of meaning all around us. If our power to recognize meaning and mystery should fail, if our imagination (in which we put our faith), our most profound and vital faculty, is crippled—then we are lost and will plunge like Icarus as he soared toward the sun.

When *Maya* was published, a reviewer wrote that it would take European readers a whole generation to digest this book. In its recognition of the work's importance, the comment is accurate, but in its good opinion of the Europe of our day, questionable. One thing is, however, certain. For those who were privileged to know him, the memory of Heinrich Zimmer lives on: the memory of a manner that was sublimely unprofessorial, the memory of his caustic wit, the fire of his spirited conversation, the dazzling intellectual thunderbolts flashing through the cloudbursts of his talk, the sparkling aperçus, the profound illuminations—his capacity for truly hearty laughter, when that sovereign spirit of his would sweep out triumphantly over the deep melancholy of his worldview. And finally, when his conversation was getting close to the realm of the unutterable, his silences—still eloquent with the expressive gestures of a man who always found his greatest happiness in words.

3

ZIMMER AND THE MELLONS

William McGuire

M ARY AND PAUL MELLON became Jungian analysands, in a manner of speaking, when they began having analytical interviews with Ann and Erlo van Waveren in New York City. That was in 1935, soon after the Mellons' marriage. While the van Waverens' credentials as analytical psychologists were obscure (there was no formal training program in those days, and it is difficult to ascertain whether they trained in any sense with either Jung himself or any of his disciples), they had been involved with Olga Froebe-Kapteyn, the founder of the Eranos conferences near Ascona, in the Italian-speaking part of Switzerland. Erlo van Waveren had been the business manager of the School of Spiritual Research, which Frau Froebe had established with the American post-Theosophist Alice A. Bailey several years before she founded Eranos. The van Waverens maintained a close friendship with Olga Froebe and, after setting up their joint practice in New York, undoubtedly commended Eranos to their clients.

The Mellons, who had met Jung when he lectured in New York during October 1937, were determined to work with him, and in December Paul Mellon wrote asking Jung for appointments the next spring. They arrived in Zurich in early May and began analytical sessions with Jung and possibly with his assistant, Antonia Wolff. Mary Mellon also attended several meetings of Jung's English seminar on Nietzsche's *Also Sprach Zarathustra*. The attractive, wealthy, young Americans were welcomed into the inner circle, whose members were mostly English-speaking disciples of Jung. During their month in Zurich, Mary and Paul became especially close to one of the American women in the group, Cary F. Baynes, who had been living in Zurich since the early 1920s and, while not a practicing analyst, was an authority on Jung's system and was his quasi-official translator. Mrs. Baynes's daughter Ximena, by her first husband, Jaime de Angulo, had grown up in Zurich. In June, as the Mellons were preparing to return to the United States, Mrs. Baynes and Erlo van Waveren (both of whom had attended the *Zarathustra* seminar) urged them to drive across the Alps to Ascona and meet Olga Froebe-Kapteyn. And so they did. During their ten-day stay, Paul and Mary Mellon were frequent guests at Frau Froebe's villa, Casa Gabriella, talking with her and Cary Baynes about many things Jungian, but particularly about the importance of publishing a collected English edition of Jung's writings, as well as related works: the seed of Mary Mellon's plan for the Bollingen Series. Before leaving to sail home, the Mellons promised Frau Froebe a subsidy for a volume of Eranos lectures on the Great Mother (which would be the theme of that summer's Eranos conference) as well as for a trip to Italy and Greece—"a cruise into the territory of the Magna Mater," Froebe said—where she intended to research material for an archive of archetypal symbolism that she was assembling for Jung.

When Olga Froebe had begun to plan the Eranos conferences, the first lecturer she had approached was Heinrich Zimmer, professor of Indology at Heidelberg University. Zimmer responded enthusiastically, and in 1933 he gave the opening lecture, on Indian Tantric yoga, at the inaugural conference. Zimmer became an advisor to Frau Froebe, whom he liked to address as "Liebe Verehrte Urmutter" ("dear adored Ur-mother"). His friendship with Jung had begun in October 1932, when he came to Zurich with another Indologist, J. W. Hauer, to take part in a seminar on Kundalini yoga that Jung gave jointly with Hauer. Zimmer returned to Zurich several times to lecture to the Analytical Psychology Club on Indian religion and mythology. (As for Hauer, when he lectured on "The Self in Indo-Aryan Mysticism" at the 1934 Eranos conference, he delivered an off-the-cuff apologia for the Nazi regime and later, having founded the "German Faith Movement," became involved with the Nazi party. Zimmer described him as "most unreliable as a scholar and as a character as well." Both Jung and Froebe ultimately broke with Hauer.)

When the Mellons returned to Switzerland in August 1939, Eranos was their first stop. After landing in Genoa, they drove up to Ascona and attended the entire week-long conference, whose theme was "The Symbolism of Rebirth in the Religious Imagery of Various Times and Peoples." Three of the lecturers spoke in French, Louis Massignon, Charles Virolleaud, and Paul Pelliot; Ernesto Buonaiuti spoke in Italian; five were German-speaking, Walter F. Otto, Hans Leisegang, Heinrich Zimmer, Richard Thurnwald, and Jung, who gave an impromptu lecture; only Charles R. D. Allberry spoke in English. It is doubtful that any of the lectures got through to the Mellons other than Allberry's and perhaps those in French, which the Mellons knew. But most of the Continental scholars could converse in English, and there were cordial encounters, especially with Zimmer, Massignon, and Allberry. The Mellons took at once to Allberry, a young scholar of Manichaeanism at Oxford University, and he might have played an important part in Mary's Bollingen program. But he joined the Royal Air Force and was shot down over Germany in 1943. Mary also responded warmly to the French Islamicist Massignon, an electrifying speaker whom she marked down as a publishing prospect. She and Paul were mesmerized by Zimmer, who by this time had left Nazi Germany for Oxford (where, as a fellow scholar, he would have known Allberry). He spoke a "racy, fluent, if odd sort of English"; he was, in a word, irrepressible. Jung called him a *puer aeternus*, a perpetual boy. An American Jungian who attended Eranos, Hildegard Nagel, wrote of Zimmer in a report to the Analytical Psychology Club of New York that "when he is excited or has had a glass of Italian wine, he spouts vocabulary like a geyser or like James Joyce. To hear him is like watching Shankar dance. It is mythology orchestrated."[1]

Despite the outbreak of World War II on September 1, 1939, Paul and Mary Mellon stayed on in Zurich through the winter of the "phony war," preoccupied with their analytical work. Not until April 1940 did Jung invite them to visit his tower retreat near the village of Bollingen, where Mary sought his approval of her publishing project. Jung gave his blessing to the program and to naming it not after him, as she had at first hoped, but after the nearby village. Shortly afterward, when German forces invaded Denmark, Norway, and the Low Countries, the Mellons left for home.

Owing to his criticism of the Hitler regime and his wife's part-Jewish ancestry, in 1938 Zimmer had been dismissed from his university chair and had found refuge in Oxford, where he had a year's unpaid appointment. The family was assisted financially by Alice Astor, the wealthy former wife of Raimund von Hofmannsthal, Christiane Zimmer's brother, who represented Time, Inc. in London. In June 1940 Zimmer sailed for New York with his wife, their books, their furniture, and their three sons—Andreas, ten; Klemens, eight; and Michel, six. They traveled on the SS *Samaria*, zigzagging in convoy. A shipboard acquaintance was the English photographer, Cecil Beaton, who wrote in his diary: "It is a revelation to hear the point of view of intelligent people, who were fighting against us in the First World War, discussing the present situation. . . . Zimmer, a man of intensity and torrent-like vitality, who works in Intelligence, says he knew after the first two months that Germany had lost the war. He is so robust and optimistic, so strong within his convictions, that he makes me feel like a wriggling winkle. . . . This man's intellectual range is enormous. He is brilliant

---

[1] See William McGuire, *Bollingen: An Adventure in Collecting the Past* (Princeton: Princeton University Press, 1982), 30–31.

when discussing anything from *Jane Eyre* to the 'Galician nobility' on board the ship."[2]

Zimmer settled his family with an aunt of his wife's at 186 Woodlawn Avenue, in New Rochelle, north of New York City and, coincidentally, near the house where Joseph Campbell had grown up. He began his Americanization by styling himself Henry R. Zimmer; his sons, having entered public school, became Andrew, Clement, and Michael. In October, when Zimmer lectured to the Analytical Psychology Club at a dinner meeting in the Brevoort Hotel, his subject was "The Impress of Dr. Jung's Teachings on My Profession." He began his talk by describing how Jung's way of silently pouring "a generous drop of gin into a glass of lemon-squash" exemplified the manner of the Zen Buddhist masters.

Zimmer soon was in touch with Mary Mellon, who was beginning to lay out what she at first called the Bollingen Press. She commissioned him to write a foreword to an "American Eranos Yearbook" that she was planning, and he delivered an eleven-page manuscript in German, which disappeared in the files when the "Yearbook" project was later abandoned. (It is now in the Bollingen Foundation archive at the Library of Congress.) From the outset Zimmer was Mary's principal advisor, mentor, and guide. He recommended that she appoint as editor Cary Baynes's daughter, Ximena de Angulo, newly graduated from Bennington College and, having grown up in Zurich, bilingual and au courant with the Jungian milieu. The editorial office of the press was in the Baynes house at Washington, Connecticut, where Cary Baynes was preoccupied with an assignment that Jung had given her some years earlier—translating a Chinese classic, the *I Ching, or Book of Changes*, from the German of Richard Wilhelm. That and the Eranos volume were then the only items on Mary's Bollingen agenda. Translations of Jung's works were as yet only a dim prospect.

Zimmer was in Baltimore in November 1940, having been invited by the Johns Hopkins Institute of the History of Medicine to give the Hideyo Noguchi Lectures. His subject was Hindu medicine, with emphasis on the treatment of elephants. The lectures were published only in 1948.

In spring 1941, the Zimmers, with Christiane at the wheel, set out in their secondhand Plymouth on a cross-country tour, leaving their sons in the care of their great aunt. In San Francisco they had an introduction from Jung to two analytical psychologists he had trained: Dr. Elizabeth G. Whitney and her husband, Dr. James L. Whitney, who arranged for Zimmer to give a weekend seminar at their vacation house

---

[2] Cecil Beaton, *The Years Between: Diaries 1939–44* (London: Weidenfeld, 1965), 25–26.

2. Zimmer in his garden in New Rochelle, 1941 or 1942.

3. The Zimmers in New Rochelle, 1941 or 1942. Standing:
Christiane Zimmer, Henry R. Zimmer, Kristine Mann, M.D.;
seated: M. Esther Harding, M.D. Mann and Harding were
Jungian analysts in New York.

in Inverness, north of the Golden Gate. The seminar members were part of the cadre of Jungian analysts and analysands in the Bay Area: Jane and Joseph Wheelwright, Lucille Elliot, Joseph and Helena Henderson, the Whitneys' sons, Peter and James, and Margaret Schevill. On a terrace overlooking Tomales Bay, Zimmer talked for two days about all his enthusiasms—tarot, Arthurian legend, Irish folklore, the religions of India, the *Arabian Nights*, and Jung. Afterward, when the Zimmers visited Mrs. Schevill in Berkeley, they were tempted to consider making their home there. Margaret Schevill, besides being a pupil of Jung and Toni Wolff, was perhaps the first student of the art and religion of the Indians of the American Southwest that Zimmer had met. On the trip back east, the Zimmers stopped at Taos to visit Frieda Lawrence and to meet Mountain Lake, the Pueblo leader whom Jung had encountered in 1925.

Zimmer began delivering lectures in the extension division of Columbia University in the fall of 1941, on art, philosophy, myth, and symbol in the culture of India—lectures that Mary intended to bring into her Bollingen program.

On January 6, 1942—a month after Pearl Harbor—the Bollingen Press was incorporated as the Bollingen Foundation, with an editorial board that included Zimmer, Cary Baynes, Ximena de Angulo, Edgar Wind (an art historian), and Stringfellow Barr (the president of St. John's College, where Paul Mellon had been studying before he enlisted in the army). Although he was contending with such problems as the scarcity of new tires, travel restrictions for enemy aliens, and his wife's absence some days for social-work courses at Columbia, Zimmer was busy with the Bollingen agenda, proposing projects by the art historian Meyer Schapiro, the critic William Troy, and himself—a "Manual of Indian Art," which was the germ of *The Art of Indian Asia*. A fragment of still another prospective work, entitled "The Mahatmas—An Introduction to India's Wisdom," survives in the Bollingen archives. To Ximena de Angulo, regarding her editing of an Eranos paper of his, he wrote: "You really did a marvelous job in streamlining this essay, in arranging this Wagnerian rhapsody for a string quartet. How these gods have been slenderized: it is OUR LADY MAYA in slacks walking down the Avenue!"

In May, however, the foundation's lawyers informed Mary Mellon that, on the advice of the Federal Bureau of Investigation, all its activities abroad must cease "unequivocally" because of its contacts with parties in neutral Switzerland, conceived of as a nest of espionage. Mary, citing the Trading with the Enemy Act, wrote the bad news to Jung, who passed it on to Olga Froebe with the comment, "A message from Job, which was to be expected." Mary's relations with Jung were never again the same.

A month later, the foundation's lawyers, in their caution, decided that the foundation must be liquidated entirely, although "following the termination of the war" it might be revived. Zimmer took the news philosophically. He told Mary that a lull in their work was in harmony with the Tao and had the endorsement of the *I Ching*. Quietly, he continued to bring promising prospects to Mary's attention. One was Joseph Campbell, who had turned up in the audience of his Columbia lectures—"a clever and intuitive young Irishman, . . . who knows a lot about [American] Indian stuff," and whom, later on, Zimmer unsuccessfully urged Mary to appoint as her Bollingen Series editor. Others were the art historian Ananda K. Coomaraswamy, at Harvard, "the only man in my field who, whenever I read a paper of his, gives me a genuine inferiority complex"; and Zimmer's former colleague at Heidelberg, the art historian Karl Lehmann, at New York University, who before the war had been excavating an ancient religious shrine on the Greek island of Samothrace.

In June 1942 the Zimmer family rented a cottage on Cape Cod near the beach in Truro (where the Coast Guard looked suspiciously at these "enemy aliens" but left them alone). Zimmer wrote Ximena de Angulo: "Every time I write the address Bollingen Foundation, it reminds me of a pleasant place on the Hauptstrasse in Heidelberg, an old and decent winery & butchery: BOLLINGERS METZGEREI UND WEIN-WIRTSCHAFT, where in those olde tymes you got the best steak, meat, sausage, wide and far around, and a good vintage from nearby (Pfalz). I take that as a most auspicious omen."

In early 1943 the dormant Bollingen Series was revived as an activity of the Old Dominion Foundation, which Paul Mellon had set up in 1941. Mary Mellon rejected a scheme for publication by Yale University Press, much favored by the lawyers but not at all her dish, and turned to Zimmer for encouragement. On February 7 he wrote her:

> Many thanks for your dear letter. I feel gnawed that I answer it so late, but these last weeks were crowded with all kind of business, end and begining of terms, additional lectures at Columbia College etc. Besides, I had in mind to let you have with this letter kind of an outline of a practical and rather funny aspect of the playing card symbolism, and which became most vividly alive when Maud Oakes showed me her own set of cards which she uses for casting the oracle. . . . We had a grand time together, Miss Oakes and I,—she plans kind of a little group which would be interested in informal lectures on cards and symbolism.

"By the way," Zimmer went on, "I could name you an editor who might perfectly suit your purposes. It is Kurt Wolff. I feel his kind of editing and his kind of shop would be the right thing for your plan." Wolff, a distinguished publisher in pre-Nazi Germany, and his wife, Helen, had reached New York as exiles in March 1941. In February 1942 the Wolffs had found the backing to establish Pantheon Books, which began publishing a list that the literary historian Hellmut Lehmann-Haupt called "of unquestionable cultural value," every book of which was "of decided artistic significance, or a genuine attempt to contribute to the solution of the intellectual and spiritual dilemma of these difficult years."[3] Zimmer and Wolff had, of course, been friends in Germany. Mary Mellon and Kurt Wolff reached quick agreement that Pantheon Books would publish the Bollingen Series.

It was Zimmer who guided Mary Mellon's decision to publish a Navaho war ceremonial as the first number of Bollingen Series. The story begins with the artist Maud Oakes herself, who during the 1930s had come to know Mary Mellon in the New York art world. Oakes's interest was not so much in Jungian psychology as in primitive art and symbolism. In 1941 Maud was a guest at a dinner party the Mellons gave for Olga Froebe, who had flown the Clipper to the United States to pursue her search for archetypal pictures in various archives. (Zimmer, away on his coast-to-coast motor trip, missed the occasion.) When Frau Froebe declared, "I don't understand you Americans. You don't know your own heritage. You know nothing about the American Indians!" Maud resolved on the spot to go and work with the Navaho. With a small stipend from the Mellons (making her the first Bollingen fellow) she was able to spend more than a year on a reservation in New Mexico. She won the confidence of the Navaho medicine men and was allowed to attend rituals and copy the sandpaintings that accompany them. From the words of one medicine man, Jeff King, she recorded the Blessing Ceremony performed over Navaho warriors going into battle. When she brought back her notes, including the sandpaintings that she had copied in crayon on sheets of brown paper, Mary Mellon sent it all to Zimmer, who replied (in his letter of February 7, 1943):

> Wouldn't that be the finest start for the Series dealing with pictorial symbolism, because this stuff has grown in this country and appeals deeply to the American romanticism and nostalgia of the Unconscious. After the local home and household gods are duly propitiated by this homage, they

[3] Hellmut Lehmann-Haupt, *The Book in America*, 2d ed. (New York: Bowker, 1951), 352–53.

will find more acceptable your branching out to the symbolism of other fields: China, India, Christianity, Tarot. Besides, a book on the Red Indians draws more attention from the press and the scholars who shrink from what they call *"esoterism."*

Zimmer furthermore urged Mary to include, along with Maud Oakes's copies of the sandpaintings and her transcript of Jeff King's account of the ceremonial, a scholarly commentary on the Navaho myth from the viewpoint of comparative mythology by his pupil Joseph Campbell. Thus was born Bollingen Series I: *Where the Two Came to Their Father: A Navaho War Ceremonial.*

Zimmer's stipend at Columbia was barely adequate, and money problems chronically beset the family. When the Mellons offered to help out, Zimmer replied to Mary (in the same letter), "It is very sweet of both of you to inquire about my going on at Columbia and to offer me your generous help. . . . Psychologically, for building up the morale of Dame Columbia and her sense of responsibility, I feel it would be better if no generous sponsor should show up now to support me, in order not to make it a habit that this (rather successful) lecturer is available to Columbia largely on private means. They shall have to become familiar with the fact that they have to support me, decently, if modestly." And a little later he wrote her, "There will be quite a wave, a high tide of symbolism and mythology in the next years. Wherever I look I see symptoms of this turn. The Mellon Foundation could not come in more timely. It will command an increasing audience from the very beginning and make many people aware of things they were looking for all the while without knowing it."

Maud Oakes and Zimmer became friends, and he began giving what was to be the series of lectures that she had planned, on the symbolism of the tarot cards, to a small group at her apartment in New York. In early March 1943 Zimmer insisted on coming down from New Rochelle to lecture, despite a ferocious cold. Pneumonia developed, and a few days later, on March 20, Heinrich Zimmer was dead at 52. His grave is in a New Rochelle cemetery.

When *Where the Two Came to Their Father* was published at the end of 1943, it was dedicated to the memory of Zimmer, "who was so greatly instrumental in the founding of the Bollingen Series, and whose generous advice and help will be missed by those who carry it forward."

The Mellons undertook to provide for the education of Zimmer's three sons, and the family moved into Manhattan, to an apartment at Riverside Drive and 101st Street. The boys attended the Lincoln School, further uptown, while their mother continued to work toward her master's degree in social work at Columbia. When Mary Mellon declared her resolve to see Zimmer's unfinished works published in the Bollingen Series, Christiane Zimmer asked Joseph Campbell to take on the editorial responsibility. Campbell, on an extended Bollingen fellowship, shaped Zimmer's lecture notes and fragmentary manuscripts, in German and English, into four volumes on the mythology, philosophy, and art of India that made Zimmer's name renowned years after his death.

Mary Mellon died suddenly on October 11, 1946. Paul Mellon and John D. Barrett, who became the directing editor of the Series, carried on the programs of the Bollingen Foundation, much as Mary had planned them, until the late 1960s, when the Bollingen Series was given to Princeton University Press to complete, and the foundation's other activities were brought to a gradual close. Paul Mellon continued to look after the education of Zimmer's sons, who as they grew up came to know him as a friend. Andrew Zimmer graduated from Harvard and went on to a law degree there; he practices law in Washington. Clement went to the University of Chicago and enrolled in the "great books" program, and then went to Oxford University, where he died in an accidental fall. Michael earned a degree in architecture from Harvard and pursues his profession in New York. Christiane Zimmer had a fulfilling career in social work with the Community Service Society in New York. She died in 1987.

Heinrich Zimmer's influences on the Bollingen Series list are manifold. Above all, there are the four volumes of his posthuma edited by Joseph Campbell, and Campbell's own work, including *The Hero with a Thousand Faces* (begun in a pre-Zimmer period but later illuminated with citations of Zimmer's works) and *The Mythic Image*, which carries the final number, one hundred, in the Bollingen Series, though published in 1974. The papers from the Eranos yearbooks, six volumes edited by Campbell, were originally shepherded by Zimmer. Maud Oakes's *Where the Two Came to Their Father*, whose history has been traced, has appeared in the Series in three successive editions. Zimmer encouraged Cary Baynes's work of translating the *I Ching* at times when her psychic energy flagged. He introduced the name of Karl Lehmann at an early moment, with the result that eight volumes of *Samothrace*, edited by Karl Lehmann and Phyllis Williams Lehmann, have appeared, and others are in preparation. Zimmer also put forward the name of A. K. Coomaraswamy, which stayed on the agenda until the publication of his selected papers in 1977, edited by Roger Lipsey. In a turnabout, Coomaraswamy assisted Campbell in the annotation of the Zimmer volumes.

Another long sleeper: Zimmer urged the work of the Swiss mythologist Johann Jacob Bachofen on Mary Mellon in 1942 and enlisted the interest of Karl Lehmann and Kurt Wolff. A selection from Bachofen's writings, *Myth, Religion, and Mother Right*, introduced by George Boas and Joseph Campbell, was finally published in 1967. When the work of the great German literary scholar Ernst Robert Curtius came to the attention of the foundation in 1949, his old friendship with Zimmer at Heidelberg helped to focus interest, resulting in the publication of Willard R. Trask's translation of *European Literature and the Latin Middle Ages* in 1953. A similar serendipity helped make a place in the Series for three volumes of Hugo von Hofmannsthal's writings, first proposed by Hermann Broch in 1947. Zimmer, whose wife Christiane was Hofmannsthal's daughter, would not have suggested a project so close to himself. The centerpiece of the edition was Hofmannsthal's unfinished novel *Andreas* (whose namesake was Zimmer's son Andrew). The notes and drafts for *Andreas* had been edited posthumously for publication in Germany by Heinrich Zimmer, who served its late author in the way that Joseph Campbell was to serve him. Zimmer's important early work, *Kunstform und Yoga im indischen Kultbild* (1926), was not published in Bollingen Series, but (thanks to the Bollingen precedent) it was published by Princeton University Press in 1984 in a translation by Gerald Chapple and James B. Lawson, *Artistic Form and Yoga in the Sacred Images of India*. And Zimmer turns up in the Bollingen edition of Jung's collected works. Volume 11, on psychology and religion, contains an essay entitled "The Holy Men of India," the translation of an introduction Jung wrote for *Der Weg zum Selbst*—Zimmer's translation from English of writings by Shri Ramana Maharshi. Jung edited the book and fostered its publication the year after Zimmer's death. In a way, it is Jung's memorial to his friend. (Jung included a brief memoir of Zimmer in the Swiss edition of his *Memories, Dreams, Reflections* [1962], but it was omitted from the American and English editions.) Finally, Zimmer's personal library, some of it brought perilously from Heidelberg to Oxford to New Rochelle, much of it assembled in this country, was purchased by the Bollingen Foundation and, in 1967, when the foundation was preparing to bring its work to an end, was given to the Institute of Fine Arts at New York University.

4

THE IMPRESS OF DR. JUNG ON

MY PROFESSION

Henry R. Zimmer

THE FIRST teaching which I personally received from Professor Jung, when I first met him at Zurich in 1932, was not an oral one nor was it written. I was taught by the pictorial script of a mere gesture after the famous manner of the masters of Zen Buddhism, who prefer to teach without words by mere gestures and attitudes. In this case it was a gesture of both his hands and in one of them he held a bottle of gin.

You remember how the outstanding doctrine of Zen Buddhism came into existence. Once, in an assembly of monks, the Buddha took a lotus flower and, lifting it above his head, showed it to his pupils. One among them grasped the meaning of this gesture, that it contained the whole essence of the transcendental wisdom on reality. He smiled at the Buddha and the Enlightened smiled back at him. That was the whole teaching and that is how Zen Buddhism came into being, quite unnoticed, to be handed down in this way for ages.

The Zurich lake has no lotus flowers and I have never seen Dr. Jung waving flowers in his hands. He taught me by pouring a generous drop of gin into a glass of lemon-squash I had in my hand. We were standing together at the buffet in the Zurich club, after I had my first lecture in his presence on Hindu yoga psychology. I was rather excited about this privilege to meet the man who after my opinion knew more about the human psyche than other men alive. So I was eager to get his criticism and asked him naively what was his opinion about the Hindu idea of the transcendental Self, in-dwelling man, underlying his conscious personality as well as the vast depth of the unconscious including the archetypes. But he, without so much as disclosing his lips, while from the bottle in his right hand he poured the gin, with the forefinger of his left persistently pointed to the rising level of the liquid

Talk given to the Analytical Psychology Club of New York, about 1942. From the papers of Heinrich Zimmer, printed by permission of Maya Rauch.—ED.

in the glass, until I hastily said, "Stop, stop, thank you." That was the gentle and inspiring indirect way of the Zen master to make me say "stop, stop" to my own talking. It implied his advice to come down from the lofty level of my question to more earthbound facts and enjoyments, to abandon the soaring speculative flight to transcendental spheres which can't be reached by mere words or abstract conceptions.

I found my way to Dr. Jung neither as a doctor nor as a patient, but as did Richard Wilhelm, the eminent interpreter of Chinese wisdom: as an Oriental scholar interested in Hindu symbolism, mythology, and psychology of yoga. Years before I met him, when first I delved into his inspiring work on symbols and transformations of libido, I felt that Dr. Jung in his solitary way knew more about mythology than most of us.

Since my early studies in Sanskrit philology I have been attracted by the spectacular riches of Hindu tradition in religion, mythology, and philosophy and had been merged into their breathtaking sphere. I had tried to decipher the pictorial script of Hindu idols through their function of guiding the soul in rituals and yoga practice. For years I had translated Hindu myths for my own sake, without publishing them, and tried to decipher their hidden script offered by faithful tradition, enhanced by glowing colors and teeming with exciting details.

What struck me in my lonely delights was the fact that Indian philology at large rather turned the back on this field, looking for editions and emendations of texts, for inscriptions and historical details. Mythology, in as far it was cared for, was dealt with in a purely positivistic unimaginative way with no sense for its secret meaning.

In plunging into the deep sea of mythology full of monsters and marvels, one is shown a lot in roaming through the depth of the waters, but one is not taught very much explicitly about the very meaning of the features one is privileged to watch in perusing the old tradition. One has to use one's intuition in deciphering these dreams of the collective genius of a great civilization. In fact, Hindu mythical tradition, instead of explaining its amazing features to the understanding, unfolds them to the pious intuition of the Hindu masses; it impresses their imagination and guides their souls by an immediate impact on the unconscious which is stirred to correspond to the dreamlike features and events of the mythological tales as they evolve in being told.

There are many keys to unlock the mysteries of symbolism, but for each period seldom more than one or two are available—if any at all. In reading Dr. Jung's writings I felt this man had found a new one, fit for our own period. By the analysis of dreams he had got down to the very core of the inner depth, from which at all times the visions and images of mythology, the pictorial stript of its figures and epics, have welled up. He had descended to their source in the deeper layers of the human psyche which have remained relatively unaltered through the changes of civilization and environment affecting the surface of man's conscious behavior. I felt it was a master key, unlocking many treasures—in fact, the whole range of variegated mythology and ethnology with rituals and institutions, customs and superstitions of peoples bygone and present.

Here, I felt, a new sort of collaboration between modern psychology on the one hand, and Oriental philology and ethnology on the other hand, had been inaugurated, and I was delighted by the privilege to join in.

I have been warned and rebuked over and again by friends and colleagues not to make so much of Dr. Jung's teachings, not to overrate their importance. Looking, however, on these eminent colleagues who advised me, and watching the results of their dealings with the inspiring though bewildering messages of the Hindu genius, sometimes they gave me the impression of being cool hens hatching indefinitely golden eggs.

Before meeting Dr. Jung I had come across another solitary master who in his way knew how to deal with mythology, a Swiss too, Johann Jacob Bachofen, who started from ancient Roman Law and the symbolism of Roman burial rites and tombs to decipher the pictorial script of Greek, Roman, and Oriental mythology. He is the author of a famous book on the Maternal Order—*Das Mutterrecht*—written before the dawn of modern ethnology. With him I learned to read mythology as expressing in its symbols the rise and decline of social and religious orders. It proved to be a most inspiring lesson for interpreting Hindu mythological tradition as mirroring the conflicts and triumphs of creeds and social and religious features through the rise and vanishing of divinities, through the ever renewed battles between gods and demons, through the love affairs and strife among its main figures. Bachofen, however, was dead, and the major task to decipher mythology as the everlasting romance of the soul, as *le drame interieur*, as the play staged in the playhouse of the psyche—this task was left for Dr. Jung.

In him, I felt, I met the master magician alive, whom I had met in so many mythical tales, playing a decisive part, but whom I never hoped to encounter in flesh. When I first met him and watched him over a weekend I spent in his house, at his table and in his garden, in his boat on the lake and in meeting people, he struck me as the most accomplished embodiment of the big medicine man, of the perfect wizard, the master of Zen initiations.

I had never imagined to see his like. I realized the unique chance to be privileged to offer him the results of my research, to read to him my decipherings of the pictorial script of the Hindu genius by which I was spellbound.

In fact, so I had done before without knowing. Six years before I met him, in 1926, I had published my first book which, dealing with Hindu art, was the first to pay attention to mandalas and similar drawings and to point out that Hindu idols would be interpreted on their lines.[1] Quite unconsciously I had hit upon a thing which had preoccupied Dr. Jung since many years, ever since he inaugurated the interpretation of the drawings from the unconscious and, by enjoining his patients to draw their visions, had invented this most important branch of psychoanalysis, which in its turn offers so striking a material to read the symbolism offered by ethnology and the history of religions.

In meeting Dr. Jung I felt I was privileged to [encounter] an incomparable teacher, who taught by listening, and who inspired me by taking interest in my work. In the meetings of his clubs and in his private conversations I felt a happy union was about to be accomplished between different lines of research which were bound to merge since they are centered around a common topic, the human soul and its various expressions in the history of mythology and in the conflicts of modern life.

The animal, I have been told, which constitutes the totemic symbol of Dr. Jung's personality is the bear. The bear, this huge and strong animal, nimbly and quietly rambling through the wild forest, hankering after the sweet honey which the diligent bees have stored in the hollows of trees. He takes it out of their hives, as if it were meant for him, swallows it, relishes it, and walks on. Likewise does Dr. Jung with the various gifts we may offer him in the way of dreams, tales, and mythologies. That is one of the most convincing and enlightening attitudes of his: when you offer him something he likes, he takes it as a matter of course. You will get it back, somehow and unawares, transformed and enhanced, maybe while you you watch him talking to others, or walking, or enjoying his Châteauneuf du Pape, or carving the roast beef for his guests.

The most essential among the lessens he bestows are imparted without much talking, by his mere attitudes and behavings. Some slight remark, now and then, sheds a flash of light on what is obvious for the intuition, but might pass by unnoticed by mere rational understanding.

In this way Dr. Jung completely behaves like a Zen master. He knows one cannot teach very much to anybody what he is not yet able

---

[1] This was *Kunstform und Yoga im indischen Kultbild.*—ED.

to grasp by himself. He watches you and leaves you to your own way, and he guides you, as far as possible, by silently and involuntarily exhibiting his own way.

Thus he is just behaving like Nature herself which constantly unfolds her eternal secret wisdom by the pictorial script of clouds and sunshine, of the cycle of the seasons and all other features of its vast realm.

The Chinese followers of Taoism know how to make sense of this continuous revelation, by conforming to it. In the same way the wisdom of life is taught by Dr. Jung continuously through the way in which he deals with persons, things, and situations which are at hand.

We need not go far in order to reach the threshold of initiations. In fact it is everywhere. We carry it inside ourselves and may behold it in every object. The gift, however, which is bestowed on us, in crossing this threshold, consists in new means of understanding things which seemingly are far off or enwrapped in mysterious symbols. The intuitive art of deciphering the hidden script in-dwelling things and traditions is the very boon which Analytical Psychology and its Master bestow on us and our professions.

In this way Dr. Jung's teachings have opened a new era of how to understand and enjoy the rich, everlasting tradition of the mythology of the human soul and how to put it to use in modern therapy.

5

THE KING AND THE CORPSE AND
THE RABBI AND THE TALK-SHOW STAR

ZIMMER'S LEGACY TO
MYTHOLOGISTS AND
INDOLOGISTS

Wendy Doniger

THE MULTIPLICITY of the cast embedded in my title expresses my perception of the multiplicity of our debt to Heinrich Zimmer. And by "our" debt I mean two groups: Indologists, symbolized by the king and the corpse, the loosely translated title of a Sanskrit text that Zimmer wrote about; and historians of religion, more precisely mythologists, symbolized by the rabbi (in a story by Martin Buber that Zimmer cited, and with which we shall conclude) and the talk-show star—Joseph Campbell, who was Zimmer's student long before Bill Moyers made "Campbell" a household word for something more than soup.

I want to ask two questions about this dual legacy. First: What was the role of Joseph Campbell in transmitting the two halves of the intellectual estate of Zimmer? I leave for others the question of what Zimmer did for Campbell, as expressed in Campbell's writings; I am more concerned with what Campbell did for Zimmer, both for good and for ill, by editing Zimmer's own writings. And second: Are both of the legacies, Indological and mythological, equally viable today?

Let me begin with the first question, the question of Campbell's role in mediating Zimmer to us. Zimmer came to America, to Columbia University, in 1940, and met Joseph Campbell. Despite the fact that Zimmer had already published widely in Europe, he was not given a particularly warm welcome here.[1] It was not Columbia but the

---

[1] This was in part due to the fact that, while still in Europe, Zimmer had written

Jungfrauen, the ladies of the Jung Foundation, who had invited him to give some lectures in a room at the top of Low Library at Columbia.[2] At a dinner cooked by Swami Nikhilananda, one of the Jungian circle, Campbell first met Zimmer, at a time when, as he says, "I knew people in the Jung Foundation. They all knew of Zimmer's arrival here. I had never heard of Zimmer."[3]

The relationship between Zimmer and Campbell was complex. Certainly the main flow was from Zimmer to Campbell; Campbell repeatedly acknowledged Zimmer as his guru. But Zimmer also learned from Campbell during their brief acquaintance; Campbell may have encouraged Zimmer to change into someone more acceptable to Americans.[4] There was as much of the chameleon about Zimmer as there was about Campbell.

After Zimmer's sudden death in 1943, Campbell collected his unpublished papers, edited them extensively, and published them. The first two books to appear in English were *Myths and Symbols in Indian Art and Civilization*, by Heinrich Zimmer, edited by Joseph Campbell and published in 1946 by the Bollingen Foundation; and *The King and the Corpse: Tales of the Soul's Conquest of Evil*, also by Heinrich Zimmer, also edited by Joseph Campbell, and also published, this time in 1948, by the Bollingen Foundation. These two books are central to my essay, for several reasons: they represent the two different legacies of Zimmer, the first Indological, the second comparative; they are his most widely influential books; and they represent the liminal period between Zimmer's German corpus and Campbell's own later corpus.[5]

Here we begin to encounter a series of bifurcating dilemmas. The first is the dilemma of praise and blame. On the one hand, we must be

---

a highly critical review about American Indology; as a result, when he came here, few Indologists would talk to him or invite him anywhere. I learned this from the late Joseph Kitagawa, personal communication.

[2] According to Campbell, Zimmer had only 3 students enrolled in his first course, and 4 auditors: Campbell, Marguerite Bloch (who helped with the subsequent editing of *Myths and Symbols in Indian Art and Civilization* and *The King and the Corpse*), a woman from the Jung Foundation, and a heavily perfumed Polish sculptress. See p. 61 of "Elders and Guides: A Conversation with Joseph Campbell," *Parabola* 5, no. 1 (February 1980): 57–65. This was an interview by Michael McKnight, the director of a mythology program at the Living and Learning Center at the University of Vermont.

[3] Ibid., 61.

[4] I owe this insight to the late Barbara Stoler Miller, personal communication.

[5] Campbell went on to edit other works of Zimmer's, such as his *Philosophies of India* and the monumental *Art of Indian Asia*, both in the Bollingen Series, but these books, which are later and pertain to different areas, do not relate directly to the problem on which I wish to focus.

grateful to Campbell for recognizing Zimmer and appreciating him at a time when no one else in America did. In this matter, as indeed in everything else, Joseph Campbell had superb taste. On the other hand, we cannot tell with certainty how much of the English works of Zimmer are really Campbell's. And this half of the first dilemma provides, in true dialectical fashion, our second dilemma: sorting out Zimmer from Campbell, like the poor girl in the fairy tale who was set the task of separating the scattered pearls from the grains of sand. Where are the obliging geese to help us in this task?

One way to begin to solve this problem would be to compare the voice of Zimmer in the German corpus (which is certainly entirely Zimmer's) and the voice of Campbell in Campbell's own later corpus (which is probably mostly Campbell's), in the hope of identifying these voiceprints in the two transitional works in which they are confused. But without embarking on this daunting task, we might draw some tentative conclusions merely by reading the two transitional works themselves, comparing them with one another and judging them in the context of our more general knowledge of Zimmer and Campbell. Failing even this, there is a third, still simpler, approach, which is all that I will attempt here: to listen to what Joseph Campbell himself says about his method of editing Heinrich Zimmer.

Campbell tells us how much work he had to do in preparing these works for the press. In his introduction to *Myths and Symbols* he remarks: "Scraps of paper, scribbled in German, English, Sanskrit, and French, were sifted everywhere into the pages of his library and files. . . . The typewritten notes had been supplemented in the classroom by impromptu amplifications and illustrated by a series of over two hundred lantern slides. Their transformation into a book demanded considerable recomposition, re-arrangements, abridgments and augmentation."[6] Campbell once referred to the preface to *The King and the Corpse*, the wonderful essay entitled "The Dilettante among Symbols," as "that little preface that I built out of some scraps of his writing."[7] And of *The King and the Corpse* itself, Campbell writes:

> The manuscript margins carried many jottings. . . . None were in a final state. Nevertheless, the moment the editor put his hand to them—co-ordinating the scattered jottings, amplifying the narratives from the original sources, and revising on the basis of numerous conversations with Dr.

[6] Joseph Campbell, "Editor's Foreword" to Heinrich Zimmer, *Myths and Symbols in Indian Art and Civilization*, ed. Joseph Campbell, Bollingen Series VI (New York: Pantheon, 1946), v–vi.

[7] Campbell, "Elders and Guides," 60.

Zimmer himself during the months just preceding his death—the book came to life, arranged itself, and developed in what now seems the one inevitable way.[8]

Now we may wonder if Campbell's way was, in fact, "the one inevitable way"; as with any myth, surely there are many possible interpretations. But Campbell was in general disinclined to take variants seriously, and it may well be that he simply imposed his monomyth, his assumption that there was "one inevitable way," upon a Zimmer whom others might have interpreted, and hence transmitted, in several different ways.

What made Campbell so sure that his one way was inevitable? We have his own explanation in the form of an extraordinary interview, in which he talked about what he did when he came to a gap in his notes on Zimmer's lectures:

> In my memory I could hear him. . . . I'd ask a question, and he would dictate. The style was his style, more or less. Then when I got into doing the big book on *The Art of Indian Asia*, I could no longer hear him dictating—that was eleven or twelve years later—and I was finished. There was no way to go on.[9]

When asked if he had a visual impression, or felt that Zimmer was actually speaking through him, Campbell replied:

> No, I'd just sit down and listen. There'd be a vague sense of his weight, and I'd take dictation. . . . I don't have any sense of that kind of spooky thing. It was my recollection of his manner, of what he had been saying, that is what I'd hear him say.[10]

This would make the works in question a kind of *shruti*, "heard" from the word of the true Author in the great beyond, like the Vedas; or at least a kind of *smriti*, "remembered" and dictated by the human sage to the divine amanuensis, as the *Mahabharata* is said to have been dictated by Vyasa to the god Ganesha.[11] One wonders if this is what Campbell meant when he said, "Recollections of conversations with Dr. Zimmer supplied most of the materials for this reconstruction.

---

[8] Joseph Campbell, "Editor's Foreword" to Heinrich Zimmer, *The King and the Corpse: Tales of the Soul's Conquest of Evil*, ed. Joseph Campbell, Bollingen Series XI (New York: Pantheon, 1948), v.

[9] Campbell, "Elders and Guides," 62.

[10] Ibid.

[11] See Wendy Doniger O'Flaherty, *Other Peoples' Myths: The Cave of Echoes* (New York: Macmillan, 1988), chap. 3, for this story and its meaning for the transmission of texts.

Where such help was lacking, I turned to the authorities he most respected."[12]

Another remark by Campbell shows how free he felt from the normal constraints of historiography: "I wouldn't have been able to do the books at all if I hadn't known that Zimmer would have liked the way I was doing it. He was extremely amusing with relation to what we call academic formalities."[13] And, finally: "I don't know where Zimmer ends and I begin."[14] That is precisely our problem: we don't know, either.

The role of Campbell in the transmission of Zimmer seems to me to have changed between Campbell's editing of the first Zimmer book published in English and the second. I would suggest that the first, *Myths and Symbols*, the Indological text, is closer to Zimmer's own work and that the second, *The King and the Corpse*, the comparative study, has more of Campbell in it. This is hardly surprising. Not only might the voice of Zimmer in Campbell's ear be expected to fade with time, but the second book, unlike the first, deals with Western materials about which Joseph Campbell knew a great deal, in some instances more than Zimmer. Zimmer does not tell us what led him to move from the Sanskrit to the Celtic tales: "We shall not dwell on the circumstances that induced me to glance from my special field of ancient Hindu mythology to this tradition belonging to the most distant corner of ancient Europe."[15] Campbell, however, himself an Irishman, cut his literary teeth on James Joyce's *Finnegans Wake*, to which he wrote, with a colleague, a *Skeleton Key* that many regard as his finest work; but Campbell never became an Indologist. Throughout *The King and the Corpse*, therefore, we encounter passages that are heavily burdened with a psychological jargon that is not characteristic of Zimmer's earlier books. Here is one such passage:

> One might say that the personalities of Lancelot and Guinevere had become, both, entirely invaded and enchanted by the powers of the "lake"

[12] Campbell, "Editor's Foreword" to *Myths and Symbols*, vi.

[13] Campbell, "Elders and Guides," 63.

[14] Ibid., 62. A vivid contrast between Campbell's method and traditional historiography is offered by the following anecdote. When Joseph Kitagawa, a lifelong friend of Campbell, was working on Joachim Wach's posthumous papers, just as Campbell was working on Zimmer's, Kitagawa asked Campbell how he managed the problem of the discrepancy between the voice of the man that he remembered from life and the voice of the written texts that he was editing. "No problem," said Campbell. "Whenever I encounter that dilemma, I meditate, and Zimmer comes and speaks to me." "Oh," said Kitagawa, ruefully, "Wach never comes and speaks to me" (personal communication from Joseph Kitagawa).

[15] Campbell, "Elders and Guides," 96. Zimmer's father was a noted scholar of Celtic studies. Is it this that Zimmer hesitates to "dwell on"?

of the unconscious, possessed and beset by a trans-personal, compulsive, unrationalized and rationally ungovernable animus-anima interlinkage. Their conscious individualities had been overwhelmed at first sight by an archetypal, rather than personal, experience. . . . They were not two, but one: each a projection of the unconscious of the other.[16]

This is not the voice of the man who wrote *Myths and Symbols in Indian Art and Civilization*. This is Campbell wearing the mask of Zimmer.

Bearing in mind this distinction between the Campbell content of the two Zimmer books, we can ask our final question: Are both of the two legacies of Zimmer equally viable today? And in each case we may pose a corollary question: How did the patterns of the stories that Zimmer selected, and the patterns of what he taught us to see in them, set the agenda for our generation of Indologists and mythologists?

Here again, as in the case of Campbell's contribution, it is a matter of praise and blame. I would argue that the first of the two main lines of descent, from *Myths and Symbols*, more directly transmitted from Zimmer, has influenced Indologists in a positive way. Zimmer chose, loved, illuminated, and compared in detail a number of great myths that continue to inform our appreciation of Indian mythology. He resurrected undeservedly neglected texts and provided us with a basic corpus of myths chosen with an unfailing eye for a truly wonderful story, impeccably translated, and wisely glossed. But this Indological influence is relatively invisible; Indologists do not always acknowledge the debt.

However much Zimmer might have gone whoring after foreign tales, his heart belonged to India. Even when he discusses Christian stories, throughout *The King and the Corpse*, he explains them by resorting to Indian concepts (such as karma and the guru).[17] By contrast, in *Myths and Symbols*, where he deals only with Indian myths, only on one occasion does he use a Christian comparison to illuminate an Indian image, the figure of Pashupati, "Lord of Sacrifical Beasts," a particularly virulent form of Shiva as the sacrificial killer of all tame animals, including ourselves. But this comparison is a grotesque failure, a perversely starry-eyed, saccharine Christian misinterpretation:

> Shiva in his gentle aspect is Pashupati, "The Herdsman, the Owner of Cattle, Lord of the Animals." All beasts (*pashu*) are of his flock, both the wild and the tame. Furthermore, the souls of all men are the "cattle" of this herdman. Thus the tender symbol of the herdsman watching his flock, which is familiar to us in the figure of Christ, the Good Shep-

[16] Zimmer, *The King and the Corpse*, 159–60.
[17] Ibid., 160–62, 172n, 178, 181, 198.

herd, as represented in early Christian art, is familiar also to the Shiva-devotee.[18]

There are two possible explanations for this rare lapse. It may perhaps best be understood in terms of Zimmer's relative ignorance of Vedic texts, in which the original Pashupati image was constructed, and his greater familiarity with later, sectarian Hinduism, in which a positive reinterpretation of this form of Shiva might well be reconstructed. Or the reference to the Good Shepherd might be an addition made by Joseph Campbell. Unless some other data are brought to light, in which either Zimmer or Campbell tells us more about this passage, it is difficult to be certain of either of these possibilities. But I think it is important to bear them both in mind when judging Zimmer.

The most important contribution of Zimmer's Indology was his choice of offbeat stories to tell. Here his creativity is immediately and stunningly apparent. In choosing his sources, he preferred to ignore the usual star players: the *Rigveda*, the *Ramayana* and *Mahabharata*, and the much overcited and overrated *Bhagavad Gita*, or even the slightly less clichéd Brahmanas and Upanishads. Instead, indulging in a kind of literary affirmative action, he rescued from academic obscurity the Puranas, more particularly the late (and therefore devalued) Puranas. In introducing the "Romance of the Goddess," Zimmer offers this footnote:

> Curiously enough, though the Sanskrit text of the *Kalika Purana* was made accessible in 1892 by the Shrivenkateshvaram Press, published in Bombay from earlier manuscripts, it has failed, hitherto, to attract the notice of the Western scholars. The following pages present what is, apparently, the first published translation of this text in any European language.[19]

And in introducing the now well-known tale of Indra and the ants, Zimmer says: "It was . . . a great experience for me, when, while reading one of the Puranas, I chanced upon the brilliant, anonymous myth recounted at the opening of the present chapter."[20] This myth was taken from the relatively obscure *Brahmavaivarta Purana*, a text that is both quite late and rococo even for a Purana, which is saying a lot.

In addition to his idiosyncratic choice of sources in general, Zimmer was entirely original in his choice of particular stories. He told how Vishnu transformed Narada into a woman when he went to fetch water, and he told two different versions, an unusual thing to do in

[18] Zimmer, *Myths and Symbols*, 171. For a detailed textual analysis of the sinister aspect of Pashupati, see O'Flaherty, *Other Peoples' Myths*, chap. 4.

[19] Zimmer, *The King and the Corpse*, 241, n. 1.

[20] Zimmer, *Myths and Symbols*, 21–22.

those dark, prestructuralist days: one from the *Matsya Purana* (another arriviste text as far as the Vedic establishment was concerned) and one from Ramakrishna, of all people—a positively heretical move. He told the better-known stories of the birth of Krishna and the subjugation of the water snake Kaliya, but he told them not from the conventional source, the elegant *Bhagavata Purana*, but from the older and rougher *Vishnu Purana*. From the highly obscure *Matangalila*, he cited the story of the clipping of the wings of elephants (with passing references to the parallel myths of the de-winging of mountains and horses). He told the story of the demon Jalandhara and Kirttimukha, the disembodied head, from the most irregular, obscure, and monumental of all Puranas, the *Skanda*. And from the *Markandeya Purana* he told slightly offbeat versions of the celebrated stories of the origin of the flame phallus and the birth of the goddess. Finally, he chose from the *Ramayana* the nonmainstream story of Agastya swallowing the ocean, connecting it, in a flash of intuition, with the story of the descent of the Milky Way to become the earthly river Ganges.

In *The King and the Corpse*, in addition to the *Kalika Purana* version of the birth, marriage, and death of Devi/Sati, Zimmer retold several stories from the *Vetalapancavimshati*, the twenty-five tales of the vampire: the story of the girl and her lover (a story which asked whose fault it was that her parents died); the story of the three pupils who revive the teacher's daughter (which asked who she belonged to); the tale of the thief, the Brahmin, and the king (three foster fathers; to whom does the boy make his ancestral offerings?); the tale of the father who marries the daughter of the woman whom his son marries (how then are their children related?); and, finally, the famous tale of the transposed heads, for which Zimmer's friend Thomas Mann produced a wonderful European avatar.

What is the pattern of these stories? Zimmer had new and ingenious insights into the run-of-the-mill cosmogonies that he wrote about. He gave relatively short shrift to the already trite avatars of Vishnu (which Christian Indologists tended to favor because of their apparent resemblance to another Incarnation). He gave pride of place to a mythology that now seems mainstream—but only because he made it so. He went for riddles, philosophical puzzles, animals, goddesses, everyday people. He liked the things that were not like Greek mythology.

Who inherited this rich legacy of stories? We did, of course, the Indologists crossbred with historians of religion. Zimmer established the mythological canon for all of us.

The second line of inheritance, the line from *The King and the Corpse*, more heavily mediated through Campbell, has influenced comparativists in a more obvious but less salutary way. Zimmer opened the door to an often infuriating psychological reductionism, which Joseph Campbell drew out of (or imposed on) Zimmer's materials, particularly the non-Indological materials. Yet Zimmer's own refreshing choices shine through the corpus. One bias of Zimmer's that is all the more significant because it goes against the usual healthy-minded trend of Jungian interpretations was his way of deliberately shunning the heroic dragon-slaying myths with their happy endings. He preferred instead tales, like the story of Abu Kasem's slippers, in which "there is more of tragicomedy than of mythological opera. And such gossip as surrounded Abu Kasem all his life, and made him immortal as a comic figure, is the mythology of the everyday."[21] He chose for us, instead of the brutal triumphs of mindless jock heroes, another kind of myth, the comedies of failure. And he railed against certain late Puranic texts in which "the old tales have been edited, commentated, and revised, by sectarian theologians . . . radically suspicious of the joys and agonies of unregenerate, secular man."[22] He went on to remark that "theologians very rarely produce first rate poetry or art. . . . They lack . . . that touch of 'amorality' which must form at least part of one's intellectual and intuitive pattern, if one is not to fall prey to predetermined bias and be cut off from certain vital, highly ironical, and disturbing insights."[23]

For in the tragicomic mythology of the everyday, Zimmer found an ironic joy. He expressed this in three beautiful passages, worth quoting at some length:

Like the human body, the cosmos is in part built up anew, every night, every day; by a process of unending regeneration it remains alive. But the manner of its growth is by abrupt occurrences, crises, surprising events and even mortifying accidents. Everything is forever going wrong; and yet, that is precisely the circumstance by which the miraculous developments come to pass. The great entirety jolts from crisis to crisis; that is the precarious, hair-raising manner of self-transport by which it moves.

The interpretation of the world process as a continual crisis would have been rejected by the last generation as an unwarranted and pessimistic view of life; the state of world affairs, however, almost forces such a conception on our minds today. Calamity is the normal circumstance, supporting both our struggle for order and our heartening illusion of a possible ultimate security. "This was sometime a paradox, but now the time gives it proof." Yet the Hindu myth could not be said to be pessimistic. On the contrary, though presenting its uninterrupted series of critical and

[21] Zimmer, *The King and the Corpse*, 20.
[22] Zimmer, *Myths and Symbols*, 179.
[23] Ibid., note.

mortifying junctures as a matter of course, the myth, in its way, is vastly optimistic.[24]

And then, a few pages later:

Life is much too horrible in its inescapable, unmerited and unjustifiable possibilities of sorrow to be termed "tragic." The "tragic" view is, so to say, only a foreground view, held by people who marvel still, unable to conceive that life is the thing it is.[25]

And, finally, on behalf of older women:

The mythical content often appears rather like an overpainted, tricked-out old beauty. Beneath all the frippery there is nothing of the reborn freshness of a youthful figure with radiant countenance, but only a shriveled, corrugated old thing with a rewritten face. Nevertheless, just such long-overripe old beauties are often the very ones to tell best the ancient tales of life; they are better at that, by far, than the young and attractive fascinators. The only problem is not to shudder at the look of them while we are listening.[26]

But perhaps the most precious gift that he gave us, both Indologists and mythologists, was the story of the rabbi from Cracow, who found the treasure beneath his own stove only when he had traveled to Prague and learned the secret from a stranger. It is, I think, significant that it was in his great book about India, *Myths and Symbols*, that he told the non-Indian myth, the comparative text about comparative texts, that became his own myth. Zimmer retold this story first in 1936, in the final pages of his *Maya: Der indische Mythos*, and drew this conclusion from it then, somewhat different from the conclusion that he gave when he retold the story on the last page of *Myths and Symbols*:

Completeness was not what I strove for; the intention of the book is to give more, through India's own words, than India herself values in them.... The dreams of the Indian genius speak of the same treasure, what is deep in us, unknown to the dreams themselves, set in motion; they are a voice from the distance, which shows us the way to something real that the things that are near to us every day bury in themselves and hide from us.[27]

---

[24] Zimmer, *The King and the Corpse*, 251.

[25] Ibid., 307.

[26] Ibid., 308.

[27] Vollständigkeit ward nicht angestrebt, die Absicht des Buches ist, durch Indiens eigene Worte mehr zu geben, als es selber ermisst.... Die Träume des indischen Genius sprechen von demselben Schatz, den unsere Tiefe, ihrer selbst unkund, bewegt, sie sind eine Stimme von fern, die uns auf ein Wesenhaftes hinweist, das unsere tägliche Nähe

This has become for many of us the founding myth, the origin myth if you will, of the history of religions: Eliade retells it, citing Zimmer, on the slender excuse of glossing a picture of Brancusi's stove in terms of the symbolism of the stove or hearth; and I used it both in my first book and in my most recent book.[28] Maya Rauch says that it is also a key story in her life.[29] For each of us it has a particular, personal meaning, never quite the same as what Zimmer made of it (or Woody Allen, or Martin Buber, who first retold the story).[30] Same archetype, different manifestation.

---

in sich birgt und uns verhehlt. Heinrich Zimmer, *Maya: Der indische Mythos* (1936), 490–91. I am indebted to Maya Rauch for showing me her own copy of this text, in which several phrases (including the opening sentence, "Alle Weisheit," and "um aus fremdem Munde") have been underlined by Karl Jaspers.

[28] Mircea Eliade, *Ordeal by Labyrinth* (Chicago: University of Chicago Press, 1982), 194; O'Flaherty, *Shiva: The Erotic Ascetic* (London: Oxford University Press, 1973), and *Other Peoples' Myths*.

[29] Personal communication from Maya Rauch.

[30] Woody Allen, "Hassidic Tales, with a Guide to Their Interpretation by the Noted Scholar," in *Getting Even* (New York: Random House, 1972), 52–56; cited, with reference to the Rabbi from Cracow, by O'Flaherty, *Other Peoples' Myths*, 139; Martin Buber, *Die Chassidischen Bücher* (Hegner: Hellerau, 1928), 532–33.

6

HEINRICH AND HENRY R. ZIMMER

THE TRANSLATOR TRANSLATED

Gerald Chapple

THERE ARE MANY Heinrich Robert Zimmers: the scholar of Indian philosophy, religion and art, as well as the philologist, mythologist, psychologist, translator and fabulator *extraordinaire*.
We can add two more: a pre-1940, "German" Zimmer, and a post-
1940, "American" Zimmer whose fame in the English-speaking world
rests almost entirely on the four volumes Joseph Campbell produced
for the Bollingen Series. Fortunately, for my purposes, Zimmer
changed his name to fit his conscious and wholehearted embrace of
his new country. "Henry R. Zimmer" became his professional name;
he signed his publications with it and was so called in his obituary in
the *New York Times*.[1] In what follows, "Heinrich" and "Henry" will
refer to his two chronologically separate identities. (For the record,
both Zimmers always answered to "Heinz" at home.)

A word at the outset about my approach. My training is in European
literature, particularly German, which is why I came to Zimmer as his
translator, editor, bibliographer, and admirer, not as a specialist in
Asian studies, Jungian psychology, or whatever. In this article, I offer
views on Zimmer and his work that are frequently based on new doc-
umentary and bio-bibliographical evidence taken and translated from
German sources. This is done in the hope that "Heinrich" will become
better known to those who probably have not read anything published
under Zimmer's name before 1941 or, what is more likely, 1946.

Another—regrettable—reason why translations are necessary in the
1990s is the increasing lack of knowledge of foreign languages, with
the result that, as R. J. Z. Werblowsky has said, "a classic is practically
non-existent until translated."[2] This state of affairs has encouraged a

For their various assistance I would like to express my gratitude to Maya Rauch, Bev-
erly Souders, and James B. Lawson, as well as to the Arts Research Board of McMaster
University for financial support.

[1] *New York Times*, March 21, 1943, 27.

[2] R. J. Z. Werblowsky in *Numen*, 34, no. 2 (December 1987): 268, in a paragraph enthu-

split in the understanding of Zimmer's work and person. My argument is that not enough is known in the English-speaking world of the pre-1940 Heinrich Zimmer. (Conversely, little is known in German-speaking countries about "Henry," although three of Campbell's editions have appeared there in German.) So powerful is Zimmer's American image—through his affiliation with Columbia, for instance—that he is still evaluated almost exclusively in terms of his posthumous works. As recently as 1987 a standard reference work on religion, *The Encyclopedia of Religion*, edited by Mircea Eliade, gave us on the whole a Zimmer based on the works published from 1946 to 1984; there is no mention of his German writings in either the article on Zimmer or its concluding bibliographic note. The following pages are meant to be a modest step in starting to put Humpty-Dumpty together again.

Biographical information on Zimmer, particularly in English, is scattered. Basically, it consists of a torso of an autobiography, an interview with Joseph Campbell together with a eulogy marking the tenth anniversary of Zimmer's death, and William McGuire's pages on Zimmer published in 1982.[3] It is unfortunate that "Henry's" own description of his American experiences and travels is difficult to come by and has not been reprinted.[4] In German I have as yet come across very little. Glasenapp's long-delayed eulogy from 1950 in the major German journal of Oriental studies is the best known of the professional evaluations, and Herbert Nette wrote a sympathetic assessment in one of postwar Germany's most respected intellectual magazines, which was able to reach a larger audience.[5] But there is also valuable information in the appreciation by a friend from Heidelberg days, the philosopher

---

siastically welcoming the English version of Zimmer's first book, *Kunstform und Yoga im indischen Kultbild* (translated by Gerald Chapple and James B. Lawson in collaboration with J. Michael McKnight, as *Artistic Form and Yoga in the Sacred Images of India* [Princeton: Princeton University Press, 1984]).

[3] Heinrich Zimmer, "Some Biographical Remarks about Henry R. Zimmer," appendix in *Artistic Form and Yoga*, 243–60; Joseph Campbell, "Heinrich Zimmer (1890–1943), *Partisan Review* 20, no. 4 (July–August 1953): 444–51; [Michael McKnight,] "Elders and Guides: A Conversation with Joseph Campbell," *Parabola* 5, no. 1 (February 1980): 57–65; William McGuire, *Bollingen: An Adventure in Collecting the Past* (Princeton: Princeton University Press, 1982), esp. pp. 38–41 and 62–66.

[4] Originally given as an address to the Analytical Psychology Club of New York City in 1941, the speech became the second of the *Two Papers by Henry R. Zimmer* (Metuchen, N.J.: Van Vechten Press, 1944) that were privately printed. Ironically, it is more accessible in the German translation that appeared immediately after the war as "Neuling in Amerika," *Die Wandlung* 1, no. 10 (1945–46): 64–85.

[5] Helmut von Glasenapp, "Heinrich Zimmer," *Zeitschrift der Deutschen Morgenländischen Gesellschaft* 100 (1950): 49–51; Herbert Nette, "Epitaph für Heinrich Zimmer," *Merkur* 2, no. 3 (1948): 436–41 (translated above, chapter 2).

Ludwig Edelstein, who played a key role in the genesis and publication of Zimmer's *Hindu Medicine*. Edelstein edited the book as a labor of love, fortunately adding an introduction that is a warm, unabashedly subjective portrait of a friend.[6] No better expression of Zimmer's human qualities, of his characteristic cast of mind and reliance on intuition and vision, is available anywhere. In what follows I will expand on Edelstein's portrait and evaluation of Zimmer's pre-American career in particular, using his lifelong involvement with translation as one focal point; my concluding pages examine some problems that cropped up when "Heinrich" was translating himself into "Henry," or when his works were being translated, as the case may be.

Heinrich Zimmer's career in the 1920s embodied the paradigmatic shift in the first half of this century from positivist philology to the broader, more freewheeling *Geistesgeschichte*. He showed a real talent for philology, following to a great extent in his father's footsteps (his father had exactly the same name—a constant problem for librarians, cataloguers, and database compilers). In 1913 he received his doctorate in Indian studies from Berlin and in October began his required year of military service, which eventually interrupted his academic career until December 1918. Thereafter, he resumed his study of philology, but dissatisfaction with the mechanical nature of its current practice and many of its practitioners soon made him restless. His genius for translation and interpretation was evident in his first publications, when he applied and simultaneously moved beyond the "technical training, no more," that he received from that "arch-craftsman in philology," his professor in Berlin.[7]

The crucial turn was his decision to shift from only deciphering texts to translating them, which thereby allowed him to replace specialized audiences with larger ones. This meant abandoning his prescribed task of editing a few obscure fragments that would have brought him the traditional academic respectability of the *Habilitation*, a story he tells in straightforward terms that mask its seriousness.[8] One sign of the "coming to himself," he tells us, was to strike out on his own to explore areas of Indian culture—myth, Tantric yoga, and art—that had been virtually neglected by Western scholarship. There followed the first of several setbacks to his academic progress: his *Doktorvater* "never forgave me and did much to hinder my career."[9] Five years of virtually

---

[6] "Editor's Preface," in Heinrich Zimmer, *Hindu Medicine*, ed. Ludwig Edelstein (Baltimore: Johns Hopkins University Press, 1948), xv–lxx, esp. pp. xv–xxvi.

[7] "Some Biographical Remarks," 247–48.

[8] Ibid., 249–59.

[9] Ibid., 249.

4. Postcard photograph dated May 6, 1914, sent by Zimmer to his
university friend Friedrich Baethgen. He wrote along the right
margin of the card, "This is what a military stare
usually looks like."

5. Undated postcard to Baethgen. On the back of it Zimmer tells his friend
that this is how he looked when "terribly hung over after a lot of drinking
and carousing" with some French girls.

6. Snapshot of Zimmer, dated November 1916. He wrote on the back:
"When my wildcat collar was still nice and new."

independent studies finally took shape in his substitute *Habilitations-schrift*, entitled *Kunstform und Yoga im indischen Kultbild*, which he finished writing in 1925. That same year saw the publication of the first of his translations.

Interestingly enough, three of Zimmer's first four books were translations, enhanced by increasingly longer commentaries. How were they received? He was unusually gifted at both parts of the two-stage hermeneutic process of assimilating (or understanding) and transmitting (or communicating), and his first reviewers were quick to pick up on his intentions and talents. *Karman*, a partial translation (but nevertheless the first into German) of the Buddhist *Divyavadana*, was praised for its "refined and polished German."[10] Both reviewers of Zimmer's 1929 rendering of the *Ashtavakragita*, the second into any European language, use the word "congenial" to describe his empathy and simplicity of diction and to praise "the masterliness of the translation,"[11] with one of them adding that "Indian thoughts really have been turned into German, as was to be expected from an author who for quite a while now has been demonstrating his ability to impart to us so vividly the atmosphere of faraway places."[12] That same year a reviewer praised his translation of the *Matangalila*, *Spiel um den Elefanten* (The Play about the Elephant), for its "thorough mastery of the material and its dazzling, graphic style."[13] Walter Wüst, although more critical, was still sympathetic and was the first to put his finger on Zimmer's basic romanticism: *Spiel um den Elefanten*, he wrote, is a "romantic book through and through. . . . What is *romantic* is precisely this: to ramble on gracefully, within a quite inflexible framework, from one topic to another, thus demonstrating both the ultimate fragility of the framework and the roving infinitude of the mind."[14] (This venture into elephant lore would come back to haunt him, as we shall see

[10] Otto Stein, *Orientalistische Literaturzeitung* 1926, no. 9, col. 693; the journal will hereafter be cited as *OLZ*. All translations from this and the following reviews, and from Zimmer's correspondence, are mine unless otherwise indicated.

[11] Emil Abegg, *OLZ* 1931, no. 3, col. 265.

[12] Otto Strauss, *Deutsche Literaturzeitung* 1931, no. 7 (February 15), col. 297; this journal will hereafter be cited as *DLZ*. See also Richard Hauschild's minor objections to the translation by Zimmer, this "outstanding man," in his introduction to his own translation of the same work, *Die Astavakra-Gita* (Berlin: Akademie-Verlag, 1967), 22.

[13] Hans Losch in *DLZ* 1930, no. 14 (April 5), cols. 631–33.

[14] *OLZ* 1931, no. 2, col. 173. Wüst needles Zimmer even more when he plays on the contrast of method between father—"the strict philologist"—and son: "Both endowed with a fine, sure sense for real facts, and yet how different is the form each sense feels is appropriate! We can be sure that the elder Zimmer would have laid out this book . . . in exactly the same fashion the son rejected. And many from the younger generation would, I think, have followed suit."

later.) Most writers acknowledge Zimmer's double gift of being able to master the field as a scholar and yet speak to a lay audience; more than once we read that it is exactly this sort of expert who *should* have been writing this sort of book, rather than the well-meaning journalist or amateur, particularly at a time when Eastern ideas were so trendy.

These few documents on the reception of the early Zimmer appeared in *Orientalistische Literaturzeitung*, a professional reviewing journal, or in *Deutsche Literaturzeitung*, the equivalent of the *New York Times Book Review*, but never in the major academic journals. Here is prima facie evidence that Zimmer's *Doktorvater* was indeed doing "much to hinder" him in his career, presumably because his rebellious star candidate was searching intellectually, spiritually, and academically for what Zimmer called "Schopenhauer's India."[15] The point is that after five years of peer review he was already recognized as a topnotch, if unconventional, translator, an innovator in the field, and as a romantic rebel who had taken his philological talents, for better or for worse, over into the camp of a neoromantic *Geistesgeschichte*.

A fitting end to this survey of the first phase of "Heinrich's" career might be the private testimonial a junior colleague in a related field provided about Zimmer's professional worth and unconventionality. A letter to Zimmer's then brand-new father-in-law, the famous poet and librettist Hugo von Hofmannsthal, reads in part:

> For me, Heinrich Zimmer is surely the most profound and gifted interpreter of the Indian mind today. . . . He knows how to grasp the enormously remote and foreign world of India with such lucidity of vision and precision of conceptualization—while placing it before our very eyes with artistic power—that he stands in the front rank of living Oriental scholars. This was also the opinion of those who tried to get him here [to Königsberg] as professor of Indian studies half a year ago. . . . In Indian studies the situation is not as auspicious as in my area of research because of the stronger resistance there of the older, purely positivist, philological

---

[15] "Some Biographical Remarks," 249, 259. An instructive example is the treatment of *Kunstform und Yoga* by reviewers. I have located eleven reviews that were published in the decade following the book's appearance: with one obvious exception, all echo Otto Strauss's first, laudatory assessment (*DLZ* 1927, no. 2, cols. 69–71), and all but one appeared in either minor journals or reputable ones in related fields, or—as did Strauss's—in the respectable, semipopular press. The most thorough is by Walter Wüst in *Anthropos* 22 (1927): 316–19, once again, a reviewing journal for ethnology and linguistics, not Indian or Asian studies. Standing in stark contrast to these positive reactions to Zimmer's first book is Ernst Wildschmidt's lengthy, belittling report in the *OLZ* (1927, no. 11, cols. 988–92), the only notice taken by a mainstream reviewing journal in the field. Wildschmidt was a Berlin colleague of Zimmer's *Doktorvater*, which might explain his egregiously harsh judgment.

school toward the *geistesgeschichtiliche*, a more responsible and therefore more demanding point of view. . . . In Indian studies a man like Heinrich Zimmer is still in a rather isolated, avant-garde position. But . . . he may rest assured that people in related disciplines are already learning his lessons, eagerly and with great gratitude.[16]

By the turn of the decade, Zimmer had hit full stride as a practitioner of *Geistesgeschichte*, as the Hegelian language at the end of his introduction to a little book called *Ewiges Indien* (Eternal India, 1930) leaves no doubt:

> Within time-bound, ever-changing India there lives an eternal India that throws the transitory one into high relief. The legacy of eternal India is about to be planted in our Western soil as a seed that will bear new fruit, in the same way that our seed is bringing change to the fields of the East, indeed, to the whole earth. The purpose lying behind our imperialistic historicism involves the task set us by the World Spirit: to direct our attention toward the eternal expressions of that Spirit found in Indian symbols with a new, unrestricted sense of responsibility that transcends mere historical knowledge—this task is the most far-reaching task of all scholarly thought. A task no one individual can be assigned, no one scholarly discipline can accomplish; a task for which mere historical information about India (even if increased by teamwork) is far too little—although such knowledge is the necessary prerequisite for that task and is ready to be heard. But in the face of this far-reaching assignment, the goals of historical studies prove to be simply a means of organizing the temporal phenomena of that which is eternally significant, and a way of labeling them accurately.
>
> A task longing to be fulfilled—and one that will be fulfilled, and it does not matter whether any one particular individual flees from this task or devotes himself to it fully.[17]

Ewiges Indien sets out to explain succinctly seven major concepts in Indian religious philosophy, but so wide-ranging is Zimmer's mind and so enthusiastically elevated his language that of his later works only *Maya: Der indische Mythos* (Maya: The myths of India, 1936) and some of the major Eranos conference lectures rival the book in sweep and tone.

---

[16] Hans Heinrich Schaeder, who at the time was teaching Oriental Studies in Königsberg, in a letter dated June 25, 1928: *Hofmannsthal-Blätter* (Frankfurt-am-Main), nos. 31–32 (1985): 26–27.

[17] Heinrich Zimmer, *Ewiges Indien: Leitmotive indischen Daseins* (Potsdam: Müller & Kiepenheuer, 1930), 9–10. The difficulty of the philosophical language and verbal pyrotechnics probably qualify this book as Zimmer's least translatable.

It was the ground-breaking quality of the book that caused Walter Ruben, when reviewing it, to find it difficult to do justice to what seemed to him to be innovative and yet merely fashionable at the same time. Right at the start he stated that "Zimmer's book is not to be measured against the standards of our philology"; it is subjective, one-sided, mystical, because Zimmer "essentially only deals with that literature which seemed to earlier generations of Indian scholars to be downright absurd: the Brahmanas, Tantra, yoga, Mahayana are his sources." And so Ruben could pigeonhole Zimmer as a "representative of that trend in Europe today that is attracted to irrationalism, mysticism, metaphysics, intuition. In this book he is a philosophizing poet who wants to improve the world, not simply an interpreter of India or a cultural historian." Ruben ends with a string of equivocations:

> Zimmer interprets his texts thoroughly, in his fashion. . . . Zimmer's education is really at a high level for his times, even though the current sociological way of thinking does not appear in his book; his thought might perhaps be called anthropological. And because, in the end, his feelings are genuine, the book must be recognized as being good, for a book of that type. Whether one wishes to recognize that type as a type, is a matter of taste. And for the same reason we are not going to discuss whether we are supposed to admire Zimmer's peculiar language or dismiss it.[18]

Part of Ruben's problem with the book clearly derives from what Edelstein later described as Zimmer's ability to think "latitudinally" (what we now call "lateral thinking").[19] It was obvious that Zimmer had been on a collision course with the narrowly linear thinking of the old guard and the majority of his contemporaries, who by and large stuck to their specialized fields. Philosophical matters "were something for the philosophers," Ruben says at one point, which expresses beautifully the constrictive scholarly departmentalization Zimmer had left far behind. To our ears, however, Zimmer's reliance on intuition, vision, and interdisciplinary crossovers makes him sound years ahead of his time. In the 1930s he perfected a skill he had first practiced in *Kunstform und Yoga* by becoming a full-fledged comparatist, and his juxtaposition of East and West was never more systematically worked out than in his magnum opus of 1936, *Maya: Der indische Mythos*, which took him six years to write.

The most stimulating interdisciplinary encounter was with Jung's psychology, a connection that was strengthened after the two men met

---

[18] *OLZ* 1931, nos. 9–10, cols. 887–90.
[19] *Hindu Medicine*, xxii.

in 1932.[20] Zimmer's glowing report on their meeting is consistent with his later admiring statements about the man whose parallel explorations of the unconscious language of myth were such a stimulus for him. For example, several aphorisms in the Introduction to *Maya*—"myths are the dreams of entire peoples" or "Indian myth is God dreaming Himself [*das Selbstträumen Gottes*]"—would be unthinkable without Zimmer's deep involvement with Jung.[21] The whole story is too well known to dwell on, but an amusing unpublished letter throws some light on the beginning of their relationship. In late 1930 or early 1931, Zimmer wrote to Herbert Nette concerning Jung, whom he had not yet met:

> Regarding your yoga essay, you know that I don't think quite the same way Jung does, although I find his aggregate form suitable only for private or personal orientation and communication. The fact that Jung didn't get to see my old book [i.e., *Kunstform und Yoga*] until so late explains why he didn't mention it in the [*Secret of the*] *Gold[en] Flower*, which somewhat surprised me at the time, as it did him later. Because R[ichard] Wilhelm knew it, of course; and I've never quite figured out why he never wrote a single word about the obvious fact that the technique, structure, and substance of that Chinese tract can only be understood as a special Buddhist form of basic Indian Tantrism coming out of the hybridizing atmosphere of late Buddhism and Chinese Taoism. As for the rest, Jung is surely, for all his great qualities, a power-loving fox, inflated by a legitimate self-confidence because of his mind and abilities and by the adoration of devoted, big-moneyed femininity. Which is not meant as an objection. Anyone who is no longer "afraid of his resemblance to God" can be quite a respectable sort, given the times.[22]

One irony here is that, after he landed in New York, Zimmer was to become very dependent on the financial support of the ladies from Jungian circles, nicknamed with a pun *die Jungfrauen*, "the virgins."

From 1930 to 1939 Jung's Eranos conferences provided Zimmer with

[20] See "Some Biographical Remarks," 259–60.

[21] This is not to underestimate Hegel's prior attractiveness for Zimmer, as is evident in a quotation from Hegel included in *Ewiges Indien* a few years earlier where, in a similar context, God was replaced by *Geist*: "Hegel saw in India 'the dreaming of the unlimited spirit [*Geist*] itself'" (32). The relationship between Zimmer and Hegel has been acknowledged but needs a thorough study.

[22] My thanks to Maya Rauch for drawing my attention to this letter, which is in the Deutsches Literaturarchiv, Marbach. She also pointed to the twist on a line from Goethe's *Faust, Part I* as being typical of Zimmer's wit: Mephistopheles, mocking the departing Student, says, "Go on, heed the old saying and my cousin, the Snake; / There'll come a time your godlike state will make you quake!" (ll. 2049–50); translated by Walter Arndt [New York: Norton, 1976], 49).

a regular international audience receptive to his explorations into new ways of understanding myth, which proved to be one of his most positive and productive experiences in worsening times. He nevertheless continued to meet with opposition to his "extracurricular" concerns from head-shaking colleagues. A reviewer of *Maya* praises Zimmer in the terminology of the Third Reich for bringing new Indian material to his *Volksgenossen* but cannot accept his interdisciplinary forays and the interweaving of Eastern and Western materials: "But all too often he slides away from Indian myth off into general worldviews and philosophies of life. The author's well-known subjectivism finds expression right in the programmatic introduction, where myth per se becomes the exponent of mankind's archaic memory [*Urerinnerung*] and the agent of ultimate truths." Unable to assent to Zimmer's novel integration of hitherto separate areas, the reviewer takes refuge in the argument against subjectivity: "Ultimately he was more interested in the personal interpretation of Indian myths rather than in communicating them."[23] Then, too, some of Zimmer's friends, somewhat surprisingly, could not approve of a man of such prodigious expertise in matters Indian traveling for so long in Jungian realms. Ludwig Edelstein was among those who "regretted these diversions of his activity, valuable as they were in themselves. We wished that he would devote himself entirely to his own field, in which he could make a unique contribution."[24] But four books on India *did* come out between 1930 and 1938, along with a well-received translation, in 1937, of Sir George Dunbar's *A History of India from the Earliest Times to the Present Day* (1936)—a six-hundred-page volume that Zimmer seems to have translated almost instantly (albeit with his wife Christiane's help).[25]

A second major blow was dealt to Zimmer's academic career when, in February 1938, the Ministry of Education of the *Reich* withdrew his right to teach, in effect expelling him from the university.[26] The police in Heidelberg had been keeping an eye on the outspoken Professor Zimmer since August 1933 for political reasons. When the Ministry of Education pressed Zimmer's dean on the matter of politics, he reported that Zimmer had been keeping to himself, although "he had doubtless been close to leftist circles earlier." He was still permitted

---

[23] Franz Joseph Meier, *OLZ* 1937, nos. 8–9, cols. 548–50.

[24] *Hindu Medicine*, xxii–xxiii.

[25] The translation was deemed "excellent" by Hans Losch, who hoped it would help its readers understand "the Aryan East" and solve its problems: *OLZ* 1938, no. 2, cols. 119–20. There were more reviews of this book (from 1938 to as late as 1941) than of any other work Zimmer wrote, edited, or translated.

[26] Dorothea Mussgenug, *Die vertriebenen Heidelberger Dozenten: Zur Geschichte der Ruprecht-Karls-Universität nach 1933* (Heidelberg: Carl Winter, 1988), 109–10. The following facts about Zimmer's treatment under the Nazis are taken from pp. 108–111; see also pp. 168–71.

to travel within Europe, but in 1936 the ministry refused to allow him to lead an academic tour to India because of his wife's Jewish ancestry—and it was the Nazi racial laws as well that finally caused him to lose his academic post.[27] In all, sixty-five out of the 201 members of the teaching faculty at Heidelberg were expelled because of these laws.[28]

Zimmer's dismissal brought with it severely reduced publishing possibilities. Progressively briefer articles began to surface during the later 1930s in out-of-the-way professional and popular journals, magazines, and newspapers—particularly in the *Frankfurter Zeitung*—on topics ranging from Indian temples to Richard Wagner to a playful treatment of Sisyphus as a neurotic. The tragedy was that Zimmer, still in his forties and at the height of his powers, was being cut off from communicating his discoveries at a time when he was profitably expanding his interests in so many directions. In 1938 his last book to come out in Germany appeared, *Weisheit Indiens: Märchen und Sinnbilder* (Wisdom of India: Fairy Tales and Parables), a slim volume dedicated to Jung.[29] His last review was printed in 1939, his last encyclopedia article in 1940. He did keep working on Sanskrit texts, primarily the Puranas, an activity that was to bear fruit during the last four years of his life, which he spent in English-speaking countries.

Thanks to the efforts of the philosopher Raymond Klibansky, a colleague and good friend of the family, Zimmer was able to take a visiting professorship at Oxford, where he arrived in March 1939, after nar-

[27] Not "because of his anti-Nazi attitude," as Joseph Campbell once reported and as others erroneously thought ("Heinrich Zimmer [1890–1943]," 445). Campbell repeated another widespread error in the same sentence: Zimmer did not hold a chair at Heidelberg but a position more or less equivalent to a full professorship.

[28] Mussgenug, *Die vertriebenen Heidelberger Dozenten*, 111.

[29] On June 29, 1938, a newspaper article, headlined simply "Heinrich Zimmer" and resembling a eulogy, spoke of Zimmer's dismissal and summarized his achievements: "His works are primarily useful for us at the present time because of his artistry in interpreting, with both wit and verve, myths, fairy tales, or the fate of the gods by enlisting psychological and ethical categories. Anyone who recently read his retelling of the Indian legend of the king and the corpse and found how his narration immediately rendered it so transparent—the strangest and most curious things were revealed in human terms that were readily understood—that reader will have acquainted himself with a particularly successful example of his interpretive art" (*Frankfurter Zeitung* [Reichsausgabe], nos. 325–26, p. 4; I am indebted to Maya Rauch for providing me with this document). The article was no doubt courageous, given the political situation; it was probably written by Herbert Nette, who, unlike some of Zimmer's other friends, obviously had no trouble with Zimmer's use of psychology in the interpretation of myths.

The tale of the king and the corpse was the final story in *Weisheit Indiens*, which came out in the first half of 1938. It first appeared in the *Festschrift* for Jung's sixtieth birthday, *Die kulturelle Bedeutung der Komplexen Psychologie* (Berlin: Julius Springer, 1935), 171–94.

rowly escaping arrest in November 1938.[30] The position was an unpaid
one, which left the Zimmers very much dependent on the generosity
of Alice Astor, who had just been divorced from Christiane's brother
Raimund. Until recently, little has come to light about Zimmer's four-
teen-month stay in England aside from Maurice Bowra's acknowledgment of the man's genius, which is quoted with ritualistic frequency.[31]
Four of his letters from Oxford and several more from the United
States have now been published, many of which document, among
those concerns facing many exiles, the shift into a different professional working language. A letter back to Germany in May 1939 reports on his first talk in English: "[In London I read] the first lecture
(on a beautiful Indian myth) that I've ever drafted in English. I had it
checked over *in puncto* diction and phrasing and it was well received.
This has really encouraged me to put together, in good time perhaps,
something humorously serious in a sort of easy-going but pithy style,
and to put it out in this dreadful child's world of Englishmen and
Americans."[32] He prepared a summer course, trying "to express familiar thoughts in English for a number of brief lectures I'm to give (of
course they'll bring in nothing but a friendly thank-you) and for a one-
hour lecture I can give in the summer term. Don't think this means I'm
somehow working myself into the system here; it's rather a kind of
maiden voyage and swan song in one before I board the boat for the
other shore."[33]

By the time "the boat" finally enabled the Zimmer family to enter
the United States on June 1, 1940, "Henry R. Zimmer" had learned
how to translate himself well enough to give three lectures on Hindu
medicine in Baltimore that November.[34] Although he had some help in
preparing the manuscript for these lectures, and others,[35] he could not

[30] Mussgenug, *Die vertriebenen Heidelberger Dozenten*, 110.

[31] As far as I can tell, Ananda K. Coomaraswamy is the first source of Bowra's pro-
nouncement, in his tribute to Zimmer in the *Review of Religion* 8, no. 1 (November 1943):
18.

[32] To Karl Jaspers, in Maya Rauch and Dorothea Mussgenug, "Briefe aus dem Exil:
Aus der Korrespondenz von Heinrich Zimmer, 1939–1943," *Heidelberger Jahrbücher* 35
(1991): 224.

[33] Letter to Erwin Palm, written around the same time as the preceding one; ibid., 225.

[34] Ludwig Edelstein, who had been forced to leave Germany in 1933, facilitated the
lectureship for Zimmer. He wrote of their reunion: "When I saw him again, I found that
he had grown much older than time warranted. The strain of his recent experiences was
quite noticeable. He was both tired and restless. But he was also happy to be free again
and he looked forward with confidence to the experiment of fitting himself into a new
life" (*Hindu Medicine*, xxiii–xxiv).

[35] See Edelstein's "Foreword" to *Hindu Medicine*, xiv; "Briefe Aus dem Exil," 228. As
Joseph Campbell remarked, "Zimmer used to give his manuscripts to his friends and
students just to have them read them over and help him straighten out his prose" ("Elders and Guides," 62).

get rid of the feeling that English was too "unromantic" in the philosophical and historical sense to permit him to express his thoughts as exactly as he might wish:

[The lecturing] is already going much better, and I feel very comfortable with it. Besides, I can clarify my ideas by talking about one or two thick volumes, and I'll pour nice old and new thoughts into them and into a new form and language, but a lot has to be changed in the process since there are many things in this kind of thinking that can't be expressed in another language—because in actual fact you can't think them up in that language. The Anglo-Saxons simply haven't gone through that grand movement in the history of thought that's so deeply rooted right there in old H[eidel]berg, and that's why their language doesn't have any direct way of expressing vast horizons, new shadings, etc., and that's when a chameleonlike, snuggling-up process of transformation has to take place.[36]

By December 1942, though, he had made great strides: "Fortunately I'm far enough along to be able to talk and discuss for a whole hour, effortlessly and without a manuscript, but I prepare every word of my big two-hour evening course on myths and symbols and get a lot out of it. . . . I'm in no hurry to write or rush into print, *for the duration* [in English in the original] of the war; in ca. two years I'll be ready and there'll really be a point to doing some serious writing . . . because then it will be readable and more cheerful."[37]

Joseph Campbell has provided details on the way "Henry" worked on those long lectures: "He would type out the lines—not in running prose, but in stroke phrases. And he would underline in red the syllable to be accented in each word. I mean he *worked* on those things, and the lectures were great."[38] With his "racy, fluent, if odd sort of English"[39] he could hold his students "spellbound," as he had done in Germany. No wonder his audiences quickly grew, and that he attracted the general public as well; New York was no different from Heidelberg in this respect, or from Switzerland, where an enraptured listener at Ascona in 1938 reported: "When he is excited or has had a glass of Italian wine, he spouts vocabulary like a geyser or like James

---

[36] To Mila Esslinger-Rauch, March 15, 1941, in "Briefe aus dem Exil," 231.

[37] To Leonardo Olschki, December 1942, in "Briefe aus dem Exil," 240.

[38] "Elders and Guides," 61. Figure 7 illustrates Campbell's point. The passage concludes Zimmer's retelling of the parable of Rabbi Eisik that he often borrowed from Martin Buber. The reader interested in how Zimmer's words were somewhat modified in later published versions can compare the typescript published in *Spring* (1941): 3, and Campbell's edited version at the conclusion of *Myths and Symbols in Indian Art and Civilization*, Bollingen Series VI (New York: Pantheon, 1946), 221.

[39] McGuire, *Bollingen*, 31.

IC. XII.

The Bohemian captain | ~~he~~ does not believe in
dreams

~~and who~~ *he,* has not much in common with the *Rebbi* Rabbi
from Poland

- ~~who is~~ in fact *he is* ⟨as remote from him as Hindu
tradition *is* from our own way of living.-

This odd man
/tells ~~to~~ the stranger from afar | what ends his
troubles |

and⌄brings his quest to fulfilment.
what

He does not mean to do so. He does it quite

inadvertently.

In the same way,   Hindu mythology or other messages from afar   are apt

to impart to us   the very meaning of our dreams

and inner voices   which send us forth on the

quest.

They point to some treasure of wisdom which our

own soul possesses   in its own home

without knowing it, |

they guide us   to inner experiences and rea-
lisations | which we are longing for

and which really are in store for us.

7. A page from Zimmer's reading script for "The Involuntary
Creation," a talk given to the Analytical Psychology Club of
New York City on November 15, 1940.

Joyce. To hear him is like watching Shankar dance. It is mythology orchestrated."[40]

Lecturing to an evening class or a Jungian club was one thing; finding an academic position was another. There are probably many reasons why Zimmer was not snapped up by an American university department in his major field (the philosophy department at Columbia was most supportive). It appeared to him, at any rate, that his newly adopted country showed no great interest in hard-core language study: "Unfortunately, Sanskrit seems to inspire people, in the first instance, with terror, but not even in the final instance with curiosity or interest. Anyway, what would an ex-Puritan civilization want with the dissipating and intoxicating wisdom of India? A few feelers by American friends in places where possibilities seemed to be on the horizon were promptly shot down . . . but nobody should be discouraged by this in this great country."[41] There is another, more fateful, reason, however, why Zimmer found closed doors wherever he applied, which may well have had its origins back in the early 1930s. Although the story is slightly obscure, and part of the evidence is based on hearsay, at the heart of the matter is a conflict between Zimmer and the man who was probably the most powerful figure in Indian studies in the United States when Zimmer arrived there.

Franklin Edgerton, the reigning Salisbury Professor of Sanskrit and Comparative Philology at Yale, was an excellent and respected philologist of the old positivist school. Zimmer, with his book on the elephant, had what turned out to be the bad luck to scoop Edgerton's 1931 edition and translation of the *Matangalila* by two years.[42] There are two versions of what happened next. In an interview in 1977 Joseph Campbell told me that "an American reviewer" had savaged Zimmer's book, but others have reported that the reverse was true, that Zimmer carried out a hatchet job on Edgerton, who would also appear to be the logical candidate for Campbell's unnamed reviewer. A scan of the relevant journals failed to turn up a "smoking gun" review, but I discovered a German reviewer who liked Edgerton's work very much and made a brief but fair comparative judgment: the books were so different that both were needed. The same went for the translations "in that Zimmer tries to do justice to the poetic aspect whereas

---

[40] Ibid., 30–31. Ludwig Edelstein remarked of Zimmer's Heidelberg audiences: "As a lecturer, too, he became more and more popular. It was astonishing to see how large crowds, men and women of all walks of life, would listen to him, spellbound and enchanted, as were his students" (*Hindu Medicine*, xxii).

[41] Letter to Leonardo Olschki, October 18, 1940, in "Briefe aus dem Exil," 226.

[42] Franklin Edgerton, *The Elephant-Lore of the Hindus: The Elephant-Sport (Matanga-lila) of Nilakantha* (New Haven: Yale University Press, 1931).

Edgerton prefers a literal rendition."[43] A partial solution to the riddle
lies, I think, in a more obvious place: Edgerton's own book, which contains a two-page (and dozen-footnote) evaluation excoriating Zimmer's work, conceding merely that Zimmer's summary of a secondary
source and his "collection of European traditions and fancies relating
to the elephant" were useful. I quote extensively to illustrate the thrust
of Edgerton's criticism:

> When I began this work, and, indeed, until the first draft of my transla-
> tion was completed, no translation of *ML* [i.e., the *Matangalila*] (or of any
> other Sanskrit work on elephants) existed in any language. Before prepar-
> ing my final draft I came into possession of Dr. Heinrich Zimmer's Ger-
> man translation of *ML*. I have, of course, examined it carefully . . . it does
> not diminish the need for my book, even for scholars or others who can
> read German. And that for two reasons:
> First, the translation is very imperfect. The text has been misinterpreted
> in many places; sometimes owing to ignorance of parallel passages which
> make the meaning clear, but often where it should have been clear with-
> out them. It would not be profitable to list these errors . . . and, if anyone
> cared to take the trouble, he could find from a comparison of Zimmer's
> translation with mine the numerous cases in which I think Zimmer has
> gone astray. . . .
> Second, his approach to the subject is distinctly different from mine. . . .
> He includes some useful things . . . in the *Nachspiel* ("Appendix"), and in
> the *Vorspiel* (Dr. Zimmer, by the way, seems to have imbibed the Hindu
> love for playfully fanciful terminology). I must add that this same *Vorspiel*
> contains some statements on Zimmer's own authority which seem to me
> hardly less fantastic than the medieval traditions [he cites].[44]

The tone of the passage is as important as what the text says. Edgerton
sounds annoyed by having been preempted. Moreover, he misses the
reasons for Zimmer's different approach (which were not lost on Zimmer's German reviewers quoted above), and Zimmer's sense of play
(*Spiel*, the first word in Zimmer's title) is equally lost on Edgerton, who
mistranslates *Nachspiel*, "postlude," which of course echoes the prelude
(*Vorspiel*). Finally, he repeatedly labels Zimmer's interpretations as
"fantastic" flights of the imagination. Edgerton was clearly the pains-

---

[43] Hermann Weller, *OLZ* 1933, no. 7, col. 450. W. Norman Brown's not very enthusiastic review of Edgerton's book aserts that the newer text is reliable, "displacing the translation by Zimmer," while also putting its finger on the limited scope of Edgerton's text:
"There is no effort to exploit the abundant material on the elephant in literature, religion, folk magic"—precisely Zimmer's forte (*Journal of the American Oriental Society* 52
(1932): 89).

[44] Edgerton, *Elephant-Lore*, xiii–xiv.

taking philologist at work establishing a translated text; Zimmer, however, made no similar claims for his translation, which derived from a
different purpose: "I felt the necessity of balancing my interest in transcendental wisdom by knowledge of the realistic approach to life's experiences in the Indian tradition."[45]

Zimmer avoided a public counterattack, which would no doubt
have led to yet another *Professorenstreit*, a "professorial quarrel," but—
and here Zimmer might have contributed to his own harm—Campbell
informed me that Zimmer wrote Edgerton a letter in which Zimmer
was supposed to have said something along these lines: "Because of
this terrible thing you have done, I am putting the curse of the elephant on you." It appears that, when Zimmer needed a job about nine
years later, Edgerton, elephantlike, did not forget. As Campbell told it,
Edgerton used his influence to see that doors in Zimmer's main sub-
jects stayed closed. It is not surprising that Zimmer, after giving three
lectures at the Yale Art Gallery on symbolism in Indian art, would
write: "Thank heavens the Departements [*sic*] are so independent that
my rather cool and dreadfully positivistic College [*sic*] Edgerton finds
out nothing about these events and isn't even asked."[46] Even if the
story of the curse is not true, there was probably enough antipathy, on
Edgerton's part at least, to ensure that things would have turned out
the same way. At any rate, this final clash between one more positivist
and Zimmer, the postgraduate *Geistesgeschichtler* (with advanced work
in analytical psychology), marked the third major blow to his career.

And so Zimmer had to harness his proverbial energy and uncom-
plaining cheerfulness to scramble for part-time academic jobs and
guest lectures, to start establishing a network of editors and publishers, and to gain visibility outside academic and Jungian circles. The
pinnacle of his public fame was of course reached with the appearance
in English of Thomas Mann's *Die vertauschten Köpfe* (The Transposed
Heads) and the publicity he received as the provider of Mann's main
sources. For a *Time* magazine review of Mann's work he delivered a
fine one-liner: "It is as if Hindemith composed a one-act opera, avail-
ing himself of the motifs from *The Twilight of the Gods*."[47] But the pub-

[45] "Some Biographical Remarks," 256.
[46] Letter to Leonardo Olschki, December 1942, in "Briefe aus dem Exil," 240.
[47] *Time*, June 9, 1941, 94. There is an earlier draft, as it were, of this comparison in a
delightful letter written about six months earlier: "That dear clever Th[omas] Budden-
brook [i.e., Mann] has made an enchanting novela out of an Indian story he found in
abbreviated form in the 1938 Eranos Yearbook on pages 177–179. He took a thousand
little details and profound thoughts from *Maya* and this Eranos lecture and simply, in
part word for word, made a hash out of them, as if a modern Offenbach created a profoundly meaningful burlesque, a richly allusive joke simply out of nothing but solemnly
serious motifs from *Tristan* and the *Ring*. Naturally I think it's enormously funny that

licity also made him uneasy in one respect: he wrote to his mother-in-law that Mann's efforts were "a great honor for which I suppose the Nazis will take away my citizenship."[48] They didn't.

On the bread-and-butter academic side, he had become, by the semester before his death, "a proper *commuter*, with two hours of *Far Eastern Religions* (India, China, Japan) with the Barnard *Girls*, and 3 hours for 5 weeks *India's Civilization* in a *5-men-team travelogue*, which is supposed to take the Columbia College *Boys* (12) from Ancient Mesopotamia to Japan. They already have Sumer, Babylon, Egypt behind them, and Islam; now I'm leading them from Bombay to the Burma Road into the arms of the Sinologists" (italicized words are in English in the original).[49] The title of one of his last published talks reveals him, as always, applying the insights of his studies to life: "Sri Ramakrishna and Our Modern Tortured World."[50]

His obituary in the *New York Times* reported that when he died, "Dr. Henry Zimmer," the "ex-associate of Jung," was "engaged in translating and revising" *Kunstform und Yoga*, one of his two "standard works," *Maya* being the other. Because of Zimmer's untimely death, this final chapter of the history of "the translator translated" must center on how other people translated, published, and reviewed Zimmer's material. In the English-speaking world his posthumous fame has rested for decades almost entirely on the four books compiled, edited, and translated by Joseph Campbell.[51] In many ways Campbell

---

some balls I'd merely tossed up into the air for my own amusement got picked off in such good fun by this experienced Grand Old Man of tennis and were so brilliantly returned. I'll finally get to see him again soon" (to Mila Esslinger-Rauch, in "Briefe aus dem Exil," 228). The average *Time* reader just might have had a better chance of understanding a reference to Offenbach rather than to Hindemith. And since we are dealing with analogies, we have to wonder what Zimmer and Mann might have said about "transposed heads" explained in Timese: "Nanda, with his second-team head and Shridaman's bench-warming body, retires to the woods for solitude and self-mortification."

[48] To Gerty von Hofmannsthal, October 3, 1940; quoted in Mussgenug, *Die vertriebenen Heidelberger Dozenten*, 170.

[49] Letter to Leonardo Olschki, December 1942, in "Briefe aus dem Exil," 240.

[50] *Prabuddha Bharata* 47 (November 1942): 512–17. The talk was given in New York in 1940. The journal's editor gracefully distances himself from Zimmer's point of view: "The reader need not agree with all the views of the writer in order to appreciate the beauty of this study."

[51] Zimmer's worldwide reputation is built on these books as well: there are more translations into other languages of these works than of all his earlier ones put together. (All but *The Art of Indian Asia* have been translated.) There are Italian, Portuguese, and Romanian versions of *Myths and Symbols in Indian Art and Civilization*; Spanish, Italian, and Portuguese translations of *The King and the Corpse*; *Philosphies of India* is available in Spanish and Portuguese; and all three exist in German and French editions. Of his Ger-

was the ideal person to perform those tasks: he had empathy with the content and style of what his teacher—his guru, in effect—was saying and writing, and he was near enough to him to write down what he had heard in lectures and conversations, something no one can now do.[52] Campbell's accuracy has generally been taken on faith and reputation, although Wendy Doniger has pointed out that it is time we looked a little more closely at his work. This is not the place for a comprehensive assessment of Campbell's reliability, of his strengths and weaknesses as a conduit for Zimmer's thought, but I can offer some observations on Campbell's sensitivity as a translator and on some textual puzzles that should support the argument that Zimmer and Campbell must be more carefully sorted out.

On the one hand, what Campbell said about the spirit informing Zimmer's talents and writing style goes beyond many of the opinions, however empathetic, quoted earlier: "Zimmer's chief endowment was a genius for language, in the service of extraordinary insight: an ability not only to translate with deceptive ease the profoundest concepts of the Orient, but also to capture in a word the secret of a personality, the quality of a work of art, or the feeling of a landscape."[53] Campbell clearly saw the romanticism at the root of Zimmer's style and was sensitive to his mentor's rebellious sense of adventure. As he told me, Zimmer "was willing to take a risk, to be unconventional; he refused to be pedantic"—words that echo several of Zimmer's more perceptive German reviewers of the 1920s and 1930s. And Zimmer's translator was most illuminating when he formulated the secret to Zimmer's spirited and inspiring translations: "He determined that he would not translate anything that he didn't think he understood."[54] Zimmer's energy and seemingly larger-than-life dimensions at times led Campbell to label his mentor's romanticism "baroque": "His style used the sweep of the baroque"; "I would try to get that baroque rhythm that he had."[55] But regardless of what one thinks of his terminology, there

---

man books only *Maya* is accessible in another language: a 1987 French translation of the first half (*Maya, ou le rêve cosmique dans la mythologie hindoue*), which received excellent reviews.

[52] A particularly good example is Campbell's transcription of Zimmer's lecture notes on "Sri-Yantra and Siva-Trimurti," *Review of Religion* 8, no. 1 (November 1943): 5–13.

[53] "Heinrich Zimmer (1890–1943)," 445.

[54] "Elders and Guides," 60.

[55] The first quotation is from an interview I had with Campbell on December 30, 1977, the second from "Elders and Guides," 62; see also Campbell's description of wrestling with Zimmer's English, when "it was *just* off," on p. 63. (It may interest the reader to know that Campbell told me that his perennial best-seller *The Hero with a Thousand Faces* was consciously written in a baroque style "à la Zimmer.") In a review of *The Art of Indian Asia* Stella Kramrisch, perhaps more clearly, characterizes Zimmer's narration of

is little question that Campbell had the necessary rapport and empathy with Zimmer's flamboyant style and the spirit behind it. His readers can only be grateful for his labors in preserving what he did and to the Bollingen Foundation for supporting him in them.

On the other hand, there are problems with the editing, because it is not always clear where or why Campbell made omissions, additions, or changes. In fact, there are very few texts for which we have the German original, so it is virtually impossible to check Campbell out thoroughly, except for perhaps half of *The King and the Corpse* (1948), which is thus worth looking at more closely. Otherwise, his translating tracks are pretty well covered, and whether deliberately so is not at issue here. Obviously, in editing *The King and the Corpse* Campbell did not intend to prepare a scholarly edition, but more documentation could easily have been supplied. (The very useful index was not added until the second edition in 1956. Was Campbell sharing in Zimmer's antipedantic rebellion against the putative dead hand of scholarship and its apparatus?) Let us take some core samples from the concluding pages of the first story in *The King and the Corpse*, "Abu Kasem's Slippers," for which we have the two German versions Campbell names in his "Editor's Foreword."[56]

Campbell's German was still very good in spite of the fact that he was almost twenty years from his year of study in Munich,[57] but errors did creep in. There were common ones ("to prove his avarice" on page 24 should read "to test" [*erproben*]), but he also had a surprising number of difficulties with psychological terminology. "Fehlleistungen" clearly refers to Freudian slips (not to "failures," page 21); "unwillkürlich" is often an awkward word to translate, but "unconscious," "instinctive," or perhaps "automatic" would be more accurate than "involuntary compulsions" for "Unwillkürlichkeit" (page 24). More puzzling is the distorting omission on page 23. The original reads, "Kann ihn sein Ich erlösen von jenem Über-Ich in ihm, dessen Dämonen ihn in ihren Klauen halten?" Tenney and Braun translate literally, "Can his ego release him from the super-ego that is within him, this super-ego whose demons hold him in their claws?"[58] Campbell: "Can his ego, whose demons now have him fast in their clutches, free

---

myths as possessing "incomparable charm and baroque effervescence," adding that his "temperamental stature, however, was baroque" (*Artibus Asiae* 18, no. 3/4 [1955]: 329).

[56] Campbell does not mention the English version by Ruth Tenney and Anneliese Braun published in *Prabuddha Bharata* 45 (May 1940): 225–31. Their translation is often awkward but always more literal and faithful than Campbell's version; when the two versions are read side by side, however, Campbell's vitality and literary qualities shine through.

[57] "Elders and Guides," 60.

[58] *Weisheit Indiens*, 70.

him; can it put itself to death?" Zimmer's clearly phrased question has become needlessly obscure.

Campbell's changes, however, often do keep to the spirit, if not to the letter, of Zimmer's essay. At the very end of his version (Zimmer's text is four paragraphs longer) he writes the phrase "the hidden magician" for what had been straightforwardly translated, in the earlier English version, as "the demon behind the conscious ego" (der Dämon hinter dem bewußten ich),[59] although it could be argued that "self," rather than "ego," would have been more accurate. The point is that Campbell, by substituting "the hidden magician," is actually being true to Zimmer's emphasis on magic throughout the story. But there is no debate possible on his rendering of *Nemo contra deum nisi deus ipse* (There can be no one against God except God Himself) as *Nemo contra diabolum nisi deus ipse* (There can be no one against the devil except God Himself).

The original context of this story, and of the eponymous "The King and the Corpse," should have signaled how necessary it was to pay attention to Zimmer's psychological purposes and details. Both tales appeared in *Weisheit Indiens*, which was explicitly put together with Jung and "his circle" in mind, as the dedication acknowledges. This is detailed in the seven-page introduction, only five pages of which have been translated, not by Campbell but, again, by Tenney and Braun in 1938.[60] And because "The King and the Corpse" first appeared in a *Festschrift* for Jung, we have a second reason for not being surprised at the heavily psychological slant to it. But Wendy Doniger is quite right: we have to know who is talking—Zimmer in 1938 or Campbell ten years later. Which key statements are definitely authentic? Are the texts contaminated at crucial points or not? Clearly, some spadework has to be done.

Then there is a host of riddles and seemingly unmotivated changes that leaves us with nagging questions, some of which may never be answered. Why, for instance, does the ending of Campbell's English version of "The King and the Corpse" differ from that of the first two German printings? This is especially critical because the postwar German translations all follow Campbell, not the original publications. Or where does the word *dilettante* come from in the book's superb opening chapter, "The Dilettante among Symbols," which Campbell admits to "building out of some scraps" of Zimmer's writing?[61] The word may well be Zimmer's, but would he have wanted to fea-

---

[59] Ibid., 69.

[60] In *Prabuddha Bharata* 43 (September 1938): 447–51. "The Story of the Indian King and the Corpse" is continued in the October issue of the same journal, pp. 496–502, and concluded in the November issue, pp. 537–45.

[61] "Elders and Guides," 60.

ture it in the title of an opening chapter? I ask because more than one reviewer seized upon it negatively: Siegfried Kracauer, for example, wrote a condescendingly critical review of Zimmer's "Indologian's holiday" in which he kept rubbing the word *dilettante* under Zimmer's/Campbell's nose.[62] Nor is this intended merely as academic cavil: the image of "the translator translated" must be as honest a portrait as possible, which means the texts have to be as authentic as they can be.

Finally, what of Zimmer "*un*translated?" (Or "not yet translated?") There is much German-language material on India, including major pieces on *maya*, yoga, and myth; a spate of almost one hundred lively, professional reviews on an enormous range of topics; essays on Schopenhauer; satirical writings and rather playful newspaper articles on myth, most of them written after the Nazis shut him down academically; some unpublished manuscripts; a passel of letters. Let me add a final sample of "unknown" Zimmer, hidden away in the German of his one Eranos lecture that Bollingen did not publish in English. It is part of a long, dazzling digression on Hamlet as the prototype of modern, post-Renaissance man:

> This world no longer possesses a sheltering womb where one could be perfectly safe. . . . In Wittenberg, in Europe everywhere, a new breed of man has been concocted, the womb of ancient Holy Mother Church is breeched, the umbilical cord that bound him to her is cut, and that Oriental/Roman mother was the ultimate, spiritualized form of Mother Earth, Mother Isis, the World Mother. Now man will tear to pieces the body of his mother, Nature, and will quarry her for new and different forms of power and resources: her body, gagged and bound, no longer sacrosanct, must yield up its energy in ever-changing forms to satisfy those human demands—however destructive, however excessive they may be—that man's capriciousness or mutual distrust might spawn. In a world unbound, a Hamlet without bonds stands there today just as he did once before:

---

[62] "Indologian Holiday," *Saturday Review*, July 24, 1948: "Expertly edited by Joseph Campbell, these . . . meditations are a compound of psychology and mythology. They are ingratiating because they are not meant to be more than the musings of a learned dilettante" (p. 15); "Amiable as the book is, it lacks strength and precision. Zimmer is right in calling himself a dilettante. . . . There is a certain confusion in him which contaminates his psychological concepts and makes him undiscriminatingly endorse both genuine myths and Wagner's counterfeits. And his undialectical reveling in the old teachings reveals him to be an incorrigible romantic" (p. 16). There is a degree of truth in Kracauer's charges, but his dismissive, blinkered attitude probably tells us more about himself than about Zimmer. "Heinrich" *and* "Henry" were haunted by critics and colleagues telling the shoemaker to stick to his Sanskrit last, which is what Kracauer reiterates.

The time is out of joint—O cursèd spite
That ever I was born to set it right![63]

The present monolingual state of affairs in academe that Werblow-sky so rightly bemoaned will probably not change significantly in the near future. And so it is that translating texts like the one above becomes all the more necessary if a wider audience is to be able to interpret and enjoy "Heinrich" Zimmer, the man and his works, more fully. Some might be afraid of using biography as a starting point, seeing in it the ghost of a misguided, nineteenth-century positivism. But while attempting here to demonstrate that we need more documents on the man himself in addition to his works, I have found Edelstein's words from over forty-five years ago reassuring: "The better we know the spirit and character of a writer, the more easily can we explain his utterances, says Spinoza."[64] Granted, Spinoza's dictum might sound optimistic in these postmodern times and doubtless is far from universally accepted. But this does not eliminate the great need for a personal and intellectual biography of Zimmer—an urgent need, because those who knew him are fast disappearing. But with teamwork and diligence, and the assistance of conferences of the kind that stimulated the present book, we can, at the very least, see to it that future encyclopedia articles encompass "both" Zimmers.

[63] Heinrich Zimmer, "Indische Mythen als Symbole: Zwei Vorträge," *Eranos-Jahrbuch* 2 (1934): 109–10.
[64] *Hindu Medicine*, xiv.

7

MAGIC, MYTH, MYSTICISM,

AND MEDICINE

Kenneth G. Zysk

INDOLOGISTS have generally shied away from close examination of the indigenous healing tradition, considering it either too specialized or too far afield from their central interests. Those few explorers who have ventured into these uncharted lands were and are often unusually innovative thinkers and scholars who share the common objective of a comprehensive understanding of India's cultural and intellectual heritage. One of these was Heinrich Zimmer, the father of the subject of this essay. Zimmer *père* was a scholar of Celtic lore as well as an Indologist; his chapter "Heilkunde" in his *Altindisches Leben* (Berlin, 1879) remains an excellent brief survey of Indian medicine gleaned from two books of the Veda, the *Rigveda* and the *Atharvaveda*.

Although best known for his studies of myth and Indian mysticism, art, and civilization, Heinrich *fils*, like his father, was also attracted to the healing lore of ancient India.[1] He realized that the hitherto superficially examined documents of Indian medical wisdom could potentially provide profound insights into the thought of ancient Indians, on a level compatible with that of myth. He thus began a close study of these works, the preliminary results of which were delivered as the Hideyo Noguchi Lectures in the History of Medicine at Johns Hopkins University in November 1940.

Although Zimmer died before he could complete the final revision of the lectures, Ludwig Edelstein, a historian of classical Hellenistic medicine, gathered together the lectures and notes left by Zimmer, edited them, provided a preface elaborating on Zimmer's interest in the subject, and in 1948 published the work as *Hindu Medicine*, a title

---

[1] Julius Jolly's handy *Medicin* (Strassburg: Karl J Trübner, 1901) was the first systematic historical survey of the Indian medical system. It is now available in English translation by C. G. Kashikar, under the title *Indian Medicine* (Delhi: Munshiram Manoharlal, 1977). For a dicussion of other early amateurs who wrote on the subject, see Kenneth G. Zysk, *Religious Medicine* (New Brunswick, N.J.: Transaction, 1992), 261–76.

chosen by Zimmer. This paper uses that work as a basis for elucidating Zimmer's contributions to the understanding of ancient Indian medicine.

Working from Zimmer's published and unpublished materials and relying on the memory of numerous conversations with him beginning in the summer of 1924, Edelstein provides a comprehensive chronicle of Zimmer's involvement with Indian medicine. As in all his interpretations of Indian culture, Zimmer endeavored to understand the meaning of the Indian medical system on its own terms and to ascertain its value for mankind today. As the preface to the book states, "In presenting characteristic elements of Hindu medical tradition through selections from its classics, the present work offers an approach to the understanding of the aims and ideals of Hindu medicine, its characteristics, and its possible value of stimulating and enlarging the views of today's medicine."[2] Zimmer took a keen interest in and individualistic approach to the subject matter, and he endeavored to penetrate the surface of the Sanskrit passages and reveal the meanings and motivations that lay behind the concepts presented in the principal medical treatises. No Westerner had previously approached Indian medicine with these specific objectives in mind, and few since have ventured to do so.

Zimmer first became interested in Indian medicine after completing his *Kunstform und Yoga*. He tells of gazing at a charming hunting relief, while visiting Paris in 1925, in which huntsmen were depicted being given the deer they had just killed by the trunk of the elephant on which they were seated. "It gave me a pang," he said, "I felt a criticism and remorse for having dealt so exclusively with Hindu and Buddhist devotional Yoga and esoteric doctrines. Here I was confronted with a scene of everyday life. I felt the necessity of balancing my interest in transcendental Hindu wisdom by knowledge of the realistic approach to life's experiences in the Indian tradition. Thus I delved into medicine, the best representative of Hindu earthly life and wisdom."[3]

Captivated by the depiction of nature in this scene, Zimmer began work on Indian veterinary texts and four years later published *Spiel um den Elefanten. Ein Buch von indischer Natur* (1929), a translation and analysis of Nilakantha's *Matangalila*, with excerpts from the *Hastyayurveda*. He noticed patterns in the veterinary texts that he would again encounter in the medical treatises and that indeed provided the basis for his interpretation of ancient Indian medical science. Veterinary sci-

---

[2] Ludwig Edelstein, "Editor's Preface," in Heinrich Zimmer, *Hindu Medicine*, ed. Ludwig Edelstein (Baltimore: Johns Hopkins University Press, 1948), lxii.

[3] Ibid., xxxvii–xxxviii, quoted from Heinrich Zimmer, *Two Papers by Heinrich R. Zimmer* (Metuchen, N.J.: Van Vechten Press, 1944), 16–17.

ence, like human medicine, was a divine wisdom given to humankind by the gods, a view of the origin and transmission of knowledge typical of Brahmanical *shastras*. The veterinarian paralleled the physician in terms of his training in diagnosis and treatment and his social status. In both fields of specialization, moreover, macrocosmic and microcosmic relationships were fundamental, and experience and tradition, observation and theory all went together, with no attempt to establish a system relying on a single methodology or source of knowledge. The three-humor theory, for example, played a key role in the classification of types: the ideal type was one in which the three humors were in perfect balance, but nearest to the ideal was the phlegmatic type, which, according to Zimmer, corresponded both to the climate of India and to the Hindu penchant for contemplation and inactivity. Other factors in the classificatory scheme, including color, place of origin, inheritance, and behavior, paralleled the sociopolitical paradigm of human classification. Such systematic analysis revealed close comparisons between animals and humans, whereas humans and plants had no affinity.[4]

In his subsequent writings on the place of medicine in the overall history and culture of ancient India, in which he makes frequent references to the treatises on animal lore, Zimmer asserts that the origin of Hindu medical knowledge was not unlike that of Western experimental science. It began with the sages and wise men who closely scrutinized the body in order to understand the powers that preserved and healed it. Their observations and conceptualizations became the basis of the later medical tradition.[5] Medicine in India, however, also had a higher religious purpose. It helped to maintain a sound body, the instrument of spiritual experience through which one came to the profound understanding of one's true self. Based on this fundamental notion, Zimmer believes, a twofold healing tradition evolved in India: a medicine of the body and a medicine of the soul. The former, operating on the physical level, was in the hands of the lay physicians and was concerned with the microbiotics of the body, while the latter, functioning on the spiritual level, was handled by the hierarchy of ritualists who, aiming at the macrobiotics of the spirit, prevented disease of the soul.[6]

The Noguchi Lectures were divided into three parts and, after revision, were intended to form three chapters in a monograph on the subject. The first lecture, "Medical Tradition and the Hindu Physicians,"

[4] *Hindu Medicine*, xxxviii–xl.

[5] Ibid., xl–xli, quoted from Heinrich Zimmer, *Ewiges Indien: Leitmotive indischen Daseins* (Potsdam: Müller & Kiepenheuer, 1930), 68–69, 118–19.

[6] *Hindu Medicine*, xliii–xliv.

which was completely revised and edited by Zimmer, is nearly twice as long as the second, "The Human Body: Its Forces and Resources," which was only partially revised by Zimmer and subsequently edited by Edelstein. These became the two chapters of *Hindu Medicine*. A third lecture, "Hindu Materia Medica," was virtually untouched by Zimmer, and so unfinished that Edelstein decided to omit it in the published version of the lectures. (A brief résumé of its contents is included in Edelstein's preface.) But it seems safe to say that the two chapters of *Hindu Medicine* contain the core of Zimmer's understanding of Indian medicine and thus deserve some detailed discussion.

The title of this book hints at Zimmer's fundamental assumption about the history and development of medicine in India. Zimmer assumes an unbroken Brahmanical continuity in the development of Indian medicine from the Vedas to contemporary Ayurveda. This traditional Hindu view, which also formed the basis of Jean Filliozat's study of Indian medicine, published a year after Zimmer's lectures appeared, has remained the dominant viewpoint of most students of Indian medical lore, although a consideration of the medical traditions associated with the anti-Brahmanical ascetic religious movements of ancient India challenges this explanation of the origin and development of classical Indian medicine.[7] In spite of scholarly disagreements concerning the evolution of this Indian science, however, Zimmer's interpretation of many of its significant aspects provides valuable insights into the complexities of Indian medical lore and its place in ancient Indian culture.

In the first chapter, Zimmer offers a survey of medical thought from the earliest times to the classical Ayurveda. Unique to his presentation and analysis is a genuine attempt to understand the ideological basis of "magical medicine" and the role of medical mythology. Magical medicine, he asserts, first appeared in the hymns of the *Rigveda* and *Atharvaveda* and persisted right into the systematized compilations of classical Ayurveda. Calling this medical magic the "suggestive element," he claims that it forms part of medicine's "psychosomatic" approach to healing.[8]

---

[7] Jean Filliozat, an ophthalmologist and contemporary of the younger Zimmer, was drawn to the subject by his professional vocation and interest in Indian languages and culture. His *La Doctrine classique de la médecine indienne* (Paris: Imprimerie nationale, 1949; second edition, Paris: École française d'Extrême-Orient, 1975) is still considered by some to be the standard treatment of the historical evolution of classical Indian medicine. It also is available in English translation by Dev Raj Chanana, under the title *The Classical Doctrine of Indian Medicine* (Delhi: Munshiram Manoharlal, 1964). For the non-Brahmanical contributions to Indian medicine, see Kenneth G. Zysk, *Asceticism and Healing in Ancient India* (New York and London: Oxford University Press, 1990).

[8] *Hindu Medicine*, 2.

The principal example of magical healing to be found in the earliest literature is the famous charm for the cure of jaundice (*Atharvaveda* 1.22) and its corresponding ritual prescription in the *Kaushika Sutra*.[9] The main task of the cure is to attack the demonic jaundice both from within and without in order to remove it, transfer the undesirable yellow color to more suitably colored hosts (such as the sun and yellow birds), and finally replace it with the more auspicious and healthy color red. The cure is multifaceted, involving the recitation of the incantation and the use of numerous apotropaic devices and procedures to dispel and avert the disease demon. The patient's involvement in the healing processes—he is instructed in every step of the cure—indicates, according to Zimmer, a fundamental psychosomatic aspect in healing. The various ritual procedures, performed to the accompaniment of the charm, appealed to the patient's imagination, from which he would conjure up his own healing forces to help effect the cure. No part of the therapy could be used in isolation; only the combined efforts of the healing ritualist and his arsenal of remedies and powerful charms could stimulate the patient's spontaneous forces of recovery. In this way, the healer's paraphernalia served but a subsidiary (and, in light of modern "scientific" medicine, a largely ineffective) role in the cure. Ultimately, the patient himself was responsible for his own rehabilitation.[10]

Other examples of psychosomatic healing occur in the hymns to the healing plants found in the *Atharvaveda* (8.7) and the *Rigveda* (10.97).[11] Both hymns assume that all plants have the power to heal and that by addressing them individually, according to their characteristics and habitat, one can bring their virtues to bear for the prevention of disease and death. The hymns, which are essentially panaceas, betray the ancient Indian healer's diffidence toward and awareness of the unreliability of the individual components of his vegetal cures.

In the *Atharvaveda* hymn the plants are repeatedly praised and their divine personalities invoked. The verses containing the eulogies, Zimmer suggests, served as comforting words to the patient and afforded him every possible help in recovery.[12] The *Rigveda* hymn similarly bestows accolades on the plants and emphatically asserts the success of the treatment utilizing them: the plants have eliminated all bodily mal-

[9] For a translation of this hymn, see Maurice Bloomfield, *Hymns of the Atharva-veda*, vol. 42 of *Sacred Books of the East*, ed. F. Max Müller (1897; repr. Delhi: Motilal Banarsidass, 1964), pp. 7–8, and the commentary on pp. 263–66.

[10] *Hindu Medicine*, 8–9.

[11] For the former, see Bloomfield, *Hymns of the Atharva-veda*, pp. 41–44 and 578–82. For the latter, see Wendy Doniger O'Flaherty, *The Rig Veda* (Harmondsworth: Penguin Books, 1981), pp. 285–87.

[12] *Hindu Medicine*, 18–19.

adies. Upon hearing these words, the patient is reassured that he is on the road to recovery, which thereby helps him to heal himself. The hymn also mentions the healer's substantial fee (horses, cows, and clothes) which, Zimmer asserts, "is not intended as a distracting reminder of the bill to be footed, but is meant to act as an incentive, appealing to the patient's instinct for cooperation and recovery. High fees invariably inspire confidence in the practitioner's skill and the efficacy of the medical tradition; they stimulate the lingering, or malingering, patient to mobilize whatever hidden energies are within him, to pass the crisis and get over his illness."[13] The appeal to the patient's pocketbook as a means to engender healing finds parallels, one can safely say, in medical traditions at all times the world over.

In the later tradition of classical Ayurveda, the use of magical or suggestive elements recalls the psychic approach of archaic psychosomatic medicine. As in the Vedic hymns to the healing plants, the physician would conjure up and propitiate the forces of nature he wished to have serve him. By offering incense and reciting charms, for example, he worshiped the goddess of the tree he cut down so that the life spirit in the felled tree could become part of the potash he would prepare.[14] Knowing the life spirit of the tree to be in the medicine, the patient, assured of the treatment's success, activated his own life forces to work in combination with the tree's to restore health. Other magical charms likewise served as autosuggestions to accomplish efficacious results. When a newborn baby was given the breast for the first time, the physician would recite the following charm to promote the mother's lactation:

> May the four oceans, full of milk, constantly abide in both your breasts, you blessed one, for the increase of the strength of the child!

> Drinking of the milk, whose sap is the sap of immortal life divine, may your boy gain long life, as do the gods by feeding on the beverage of immortality.[15]

Zimmer was perhaps the first scholar to notice in Vedic hymns the importance of the myths associated with healing plants. The solemn praises addressed to the plants and their virtues are characteristic of

---

[13] Ibid., 28–29.

[14] Ibid., 105–7.

[15] *Sushruta Samhita*, Sharirasthana 10.26–27, translated by Zimmer in *Hindu Medicine*, 107. The same technique of autosuggestion was employed in an Atharvavedic incantation against urine retention. In order to promote the flow of urine a surgical procedure involving a type of catheter was administered, followed by the pouring of water with barley grains down the penis to the accompaniment of a charm whose nine verses end with *bal*, the sound of water dropping in a pail (see Zysk, *Religious Medicine*, 70–71).

lauds offered to the gods in both Vedic chants and later Puranic verses. The vegetal mythologies in these hymns begin with an account of the plants' origins and noble lineages. They often report how the divine plants were brought to mankind by a semidivine ancestor, who was the first to employ them and repeatedly insisted upon their virtues. This mythology of healing plants characterizes the medical botany of the early Vedic period and reflects a unificiation of two Vedic botanical traditions: that of the *Rigveda*, centering on the healing plant gods Soma and Kushtha, and that of the *Atharvaveda*, focusing on the healing plant goddess Arundhati.[16] The purpose of recounting the vegetal mythology, Zimmer suggests, was to invoke and concentrate the divine healing powers in the plants and again to inspire a psychosomatic cure in the patient. The therapeutic virtues of the plants and the patient's own regenerative powers worked together to effect recovery.

Mythology also played an important role in later Ayurvedic medicine, especially in the traditional accounts of the transmission of medical wisdom from the gods to humankind that are found at the beginning of the two medical classics of Sushruta and Caraka. Zimmer provides an original analysis of the Puranic myth of Dhanvantari, the divine source of the *Sushruta Samhita*, and its connection to medicine. Legend has it that Dhanvantari emerged from the liquid depths of primeval cosmic life substance, carrying the powerful *amrita* or elixir of immortality in a milk-white bowl. As disciple of both Vishnu, the preserver, and Shiva, the destroyer, he combined the two main elements of Hindu medicine: "The wisdom which increases life-strength and maintains life-length to its fullest extent (*ayurveda*) and the wisdom of cures and remedies (*bhaishajya*) for diseases and demons."[17]

An important episode in the mythic cycle of Dhanvantari links him with the time-honored Indian medical tradition of toxicology that figures prominently in the treatise of Sushruta. As a pupil of the sun-bird Garuda, the archenemy of serpents, Dhanvantari obtained the magical power to vanquish various venomous snakes. At one point he confronted the powerful serpent demoness Manasa and, on the advice of Brahma and Shiva, placated the fierce goddess with offerings, prayers, and meditation. Humbling himself, he became reconciled with the demoness and, by appeasing her, invoked her benevolent aspect and gained her favor. "By his devotional practice," Zimmer states, "he established the pattern for propitiating the fierce force of destruction by acknowledging its irresistible strength. Furthermore, his auspicious vision of the goddess provided the form in which Manasa is to be

---

[16] See Zysk, *Asceticism and Healing*, 17–19.
[17] *Hindu Medicine*, 37–38.

visualized in meditation and represented in images for worship, to avert the peril of poisonous snakes."[18] The episode of Dhanvantari and Manasa thus illustrates the close relationship between the medical and magico-religious arts.[19]

Zimmer's elucidation of the myth of Dhanvantari and its connection to the medical tradition of Sushruta accurately reflects the attitude toward certain (but by no means all) forms of therapeutics incorporated in the medical treatise of the same name. This connection between myth and practice suggests that the originators of the Dhanvantari myth (which, according to Zimmer, is an inheritance from aboriginal Indian antiquity) were an important source of ancient Indian toxicological knowledge.[20]

In the medical textbooks mythological material also serves as the principal explanation for the origins, names, and characteristics of a wide variety of substances, creatures, and practices. The myth of the *luta* spider, for example, wholly in the Puranic style, recounts the origin and malignant character of this arachnid and its poisonous sting. The spiders are said to have originated from drops of sweat that fell onto freshly cut grass from the forehead of the sage Vasishtha, who was enraged because King Vishvamitra had stolen his divine cows whose milk provided all he desired. On the basis of this myth, the compiler of the *Sushruta Samhita* explains that the spiders received their name, *luta*, from the grass upon which they sprang into existence as manifestations of deadly anger.[21] Kalhana in his *Rajatarangini*, a chronicle of the kings of Kashmir, relates that these deadly spiders were particularly troublesome to royalty in Kashmir, as they would frequently nest in the clothes of the king and, when disturbed, responded by inflicting their fatal sting on the unsuspecting victims. Similarly, the author of the book on elephant lore, the *Hastyayurveda*, explains the origin of garlic: the sun-bird Garuda, transporting a drop of the elixir of immortality, spilt it on unfavorable ground. Garlic, with its acrid flavor, sprang from the ground where the drop had fallen. Hence it is called *rasona* (*rasa-una*), "wanting in (pleasant) taste."[22] Other myths of this type, recounting the origins of diseases, drugs, and therapies, occur in most of the medical treatises, regardless of the period. Some originate in the Vedas or Puranas; others are purely regional.

[18] Ibid., 43.
[19] *Sushruta Samhita*, Kalpasthana 5.8–13. See Kenneth G. Zysk, "Mantra in Ayurveda: A Study of the Use of Magico-Religious Speech in Ancient Indian Medicine," in *Mantra*, ed. Harvey P. Alper (Albany: State University of New York Press, 1989), 127–28.
[20] *Hindu Medicine*, 36.
[21] Ibid., 103–4.
[22] Ibid., 104–5.

Perhaps the most important part of Zimmer's presentation of Indian medicine, however, is his insistence that medicine served a purpose greater than just the healing of physical ailments. Medical practices permitted the organism to experience the essence of reality by aiding patients in bringing to maturity the quiescent germ of divine being in their perishable bodies. For Zimmer the fundamental religious objective served by healing characterizes Indian medicine throughout its history from the Vedic age to the present and provides the ethical background of medical wisdom. That the spiritual goal of medicine derives from its connection with yoga is, according to Zimmer, demonstrated in Anandarayamakhi's *The Bliss of the Life-Monad (Jiva-nanda)*, a seventeenth-century didactic drama focusing on medicine. In this play, health, vigor, and longevity accomplished through medicine are not represented as ends in themselves but as necessities for and subordinate to the higher goal of spirituality. "They are prerequisites of the everlasting quest along the paths of pious exercise and austere discipline to win for man a divine freedom beyond all the needs and bonds of human nature."[23] Anandarayamakhi's medical allegory expresses medicine's implicit purpose: the establishment, in yoga, of the perfect union between healing and religion.[24]

As far as the connection between medicine and yoga is concerned, it is important to point out that one of the few threads running through the literature from the early Vedas to the Ayurveda is the concept of vital breath (*prana*). Its five forms (*prana, apana, vyana, samana,* and *udana*) first appear in the *Atharvaveda* and weave through the fabric of the Brahmanas and Upanishads. After the Upanishads the evolutionary thread of the *prana* doctrine bifurcates: one strand develops into the distinctive medical physiology of the Ayurveda, the other into the ascetic physiology associated with the key yogic practice of *pranayama*, "restraint of the breath." Yoga gradually began to embrace medical theories and practices, incorporating them into its ascetic discipline, whereas medicine remained comparatively untouched by respiratory principles commonly associated with yoga.[25] Zimmer's analysis of the close connection between medicine and yoga and of the important role medicine played in the yogin's spiritual quest is almost flawless. He failed only to notice that it was less medicine's use of yoga than yoga's use of medicine that established the link between the healing arts and ascetic disciplines.

Turning his attention to anatomy in the second chapter of *Hindu*

[23] Ibid., 72.

[24] Ibid., 61–75.

[25] See Kenneth G. Zysk, "The Science of Respiration and the Doctrine of the Vital Breaths in Ancient India," *Journal of the American Oriental Society* 113:2 (1993), 198–213.

Medicine, "The Human Body: Its Forces and Resources," Zimmer seeks to establish further connections between medicine and religion. According to Zimmer, the ancient Hindus conceived of the body as representing in microcosmic form the entire universe, which is composed of divine substance and energy: "Man experiences his own nature as the exact counterpart of the world organism; he visualized his body as enlivened and ruled by the same divine hierarchy which activates the life-process of the universe."[26]

This interpretation fits well with the healing tradition of the Vedic period.[27] In the Ayurveda, however, the cosmic associations are less obvious, with the result that Zimmer's analysis strains credibility. In discussing the three humors (*doshas*) or pathological substances in the body, Zimmer asserts that each *dosha* has its divine analogue: wind/ wind, bile/sun, and phlegm/moon. Wind moves about in various directions; the sun by its draining rays extracts the sap from creatures; and the moon pours down renewal of life's sap. Together they support the body of the universe and represent not only airy, bilious, and mucus matter but also aerial, fiery, and liquid forms of life.[28] These connections are logical enough in the Indian context, but meager support for them in fact exists in the classical medical treatises. Zimmer's attempt to find the origin of the three-humor theory in ancient Brahmanical religious ideology is thus untenable.

More valuable is his observation that the three *doshas* are usually characterized in terms of human emotional states. The *doshas* become incensed and infuriated and require appeasement by the skilled doctor. According to Zimmer, this personification of the *doshas* reflects a "pre-critical period of thought when observation and imagination combined for the purpose of unveiling nature's secret ways."[29] Pointing to the inherent anthropomorphism in the conceptualization of the three humors, he concludes: "Hindu physiology unfolds like a spectacular romance of the three humors, with their quarrels and appeasements, aggressions and defeats. . . . As long as they hold one another in check through a proper balance, all is well; the life-process and all the activities of the metabolism go on smoothly."[30] By calling atten-

---

[26] *Hindu Medicine*, 114.

[27] See Kenneth G. Zysk, "The Evolution of Anatomical Knowledge in Ancient India, with Special Reference to Cross-cultural Influences," *Journal of the American Oriental Society* 106, no. 4 (1986): 688–90.

[28] *Hindu Medicine*, 136. Cf. S. N. Dasgupta, *History of Indian Philosophy* (1922; repr. Delhi: Motilal Banarsidass, 1975), 2:330–33, where many of Zimmer's basic ideas about the three-humor doctrine of Ayurveda are expressed.

[29] *Hindu Medicine*, 138.

[30] Ibid.

tion to the romantic aspect of this central doctrine of Ayurvedic medicine, Zimmer correctly identifies one of its uniquely Indian characteristics, irrespective of where and when this characteristic may have originated.

Zimmer also has much to say about wind (*vata, vayu*) and its relation to breath (*prana*), for this relationship advances his thesis of a religiously based medical tradition. However, he is again skating on thin ice when he claims that the Indian medical notion of wind derives from a fundamental Upanishadic idea that wind is the self-existent, supreme divine element, the universal Self of all beings (*sarvatman*). Although a vague reference in the *Caraka Samhita* does suggest a possible connection between *prana* (and *apana*) and Upanishadic *atman*, by and large the classical medical treatises have no such theological pronouncements.

It is clear, however, that the medical doctrine of the five winds, *prana, udana, samana, vyana,* and *apana,* derived from Upanishadic thought. Zimmer asserts that the first two, *prana,* "breathing forward," and *udana,* "breathing upward," have nothing to do with respiration, because Indian physicians had no knowledge of the actual function of the lungs, which they conceived to be the reservoir of phlegm rather than of wind.[31] The medical notion of the five breaths flowing throughout the body and motivating various physiological functions must be viewed, Zimmer claims, against the background of the yoga system, which likewise failed to recognize the function of the lungs. During the exercise of *pranayama,* which is already referred to in the early Upanishads, the entire body becomes filled with air (as experienced in the sensation of hyperventilation). Air enters the mouth and immediately begins to flow through the body's channels, the most important of which are the *ida* and *pingala,* understood to be the two major nerves situated respectively on the left and right sides of the central nerve of the spine. The experiences related to this yogic practice provided the empirical basis for a pneumatic physiology that the Indian medical tradition adopted and modified.[32]

Ancient Indian healers knew the lungs only as the seat of fluids. Pulmonary consumption, for example, was called *shosha,* "drying up," and signified the destruction of the lungs by an attack on the seat of watery matter and the drying out of phlegm. Indian physicians were similarly unaware of the proper function of the brain. The seat of consciousness was understood to be the heart, where emotion is "felt," an idea not unique to India. These two ideas exemplify the healer's

[31] Ibid., 146.
[32] Ibid., 142–60.

understanding of the relationship of a body part to a bodily function, or, to put it another way, the relationship of anatomy to physiology. Although medical language, Zimmer asserts, proliferates with rationalistic words and phrases, the body and its operations are meant to be understood as a pictorial script. "In anatomical terminology," he states, the medical authors "describe inner sensations which were visualized again and again until they became a classical pattern satisfying common experience."[33]

Not surprisingly, analogical reasoning was utilized in ancient Indian anatomy and physiology almost entirely in relation to the internal organs and their operations, since empirical knowledge of these organs was hard to come by. For the grosser anatomical parts, however, fairly accurate descriptions do reveal empirical modes of thought that reflect different sources of knowledge. Dissection was, in fact, introduced for a short period by the classical surgical tradition of Sushruta. In Zimmer's view, this pedagogical technique had a brief life span because it clashed with the Hindu penchant for purity and hygiene, especially given a subtropical climate. Moreover, the knowledge of anatomy acquired by the ritual immolation and carving up of animals fell into obscurity because of increasingly strong pressures toward vegetarianism and nonviolence, which also grew out of the demands of subtropical hygiene. In addition, the older practice of burial was replaced by cremation, which effectively eliminated any opportunity to acquire anatomical knowledge.

In the ancient Indian dissection procedure, the corpse was left to decay in a cage concealed in a flowing stream. It was then fished out and the layers of skin gradually removed with grass brooms until the inner organs became exposed to the eye. This method permitted the visual inspection of a body that had been kept pure by running water and protected from desecration by a cage, without anyone ever actually touching it and thus becoming defiled by it. A fairly detailed knowledge of the skeletal and muscular systems would have been obtained by the gentle scrapping away of layers of skin and flesh. Any accurate inspection of the nervous and vascular systems, though, would have been greatly impaired by the physical state of the mushy, putrefied flesh. Likewise, clear delineation of the internal organs and their functions would be nearly impossible because of the body's decomposed state. Moreover, given the aversion to physical contact with a corpse, no attempt was made to penetrate the cranium to investigate its contents. The result was a reasonably clear understanding of the

[33] Ibid., 164–65.

bones, muscles, ligaments, and tendons, but knowledge of the internal organs and vessels and their functions remained on the level of abstract speculation.[34]

It is appropriate at this juncture to examine Zimmer's remarks on Indian materia medica and on Greek and Indian medical interactions, for they complete the picture of ancient Indian medicine he was striving to portray. Zimmer's analysis of Indian materia medica can be found in Edelstein's summary of Zimmer's third lecture, "Hindu Materia Medica," which amounted only to nineteen manuscript pages but was intended to be the third and final chapter in his book. According to Zimmer, Hindu materia medica, consisting of countless prescriptions, "forms the bulk of India's therapeutical wisdom."[35] These Indian recipes, Zimmer claims, resemble the traditional pharmacopoeia of Western medicine before the days of modern pharmacology and experimental chemistry. They also reflect a fundamental conservatism, whereby no item once approved by tradition was ever omitted. Instead, new ingredients were added if old mixtures proved ineffective. In this way, "the amazing intricacy of traditional recipes comes about in the course of time."[36]

Although the conservatism of traditional Indian materia medica inhibited experimentation and innovation, it potentially maintained certain secret truths from which new insights could be obtained. "During its long development," Zimmer states, Indian materia medica "has accumulated the ever renewed experiences of India's inhabitants, using the resources of their environment for the purpose of healing. With its remarkable insight into the influences of regions and seasons, diet and climate, it records the instinctive and subtle adjustment of the people of India to the peculiarities of her trying climate. Traditional as it is, and overlaid with speculative and systematizing superstructures, it contains the treasures of 'old woman's' experience."[37] In comparison to Western medieval materia medica, he claims, which were often stale owing to the need to import drugs to Europe from the Mediterranean, the Indian drugs were fresh and native and thus may have proved more efficacious. His discussion concludes with a recommendation that modern science work hand in hand with traditional Indian medical specialists to examine the drugs of the native pharmacopoeias in order to determine the efficacy of their prescriptions and

[34] Ibid., 175–78.
[35] Ibid., li.
[36] Ibid., liii.
[37] Ibid., lv.

perhaps discover important new medicines hidden in ancient medical wisdom.[38]

Zimmer's general comments about traditional Indian materia medica fit neatly into the conclusions of Francis Zimmermann's more recent and exhaustive treatment of the subject in *The Jungle and the Aroma of Meats*.[39] Zimmer's recommendation that traditional recipes be subjected to scientific scrutiny remains an urgent desideratum in the study of India's medical lore. Because the ratio of success to expenditure has proved to be very low, however, the major pharmaceutical firms are reluctant to fund such experimental projects. According to Johannes Laping, the problem seems to lie with the lack of cooperation among scholars of Indian medical philology, anthropologists, scientists, and native practitioners. Closer dialogue between these specialists, he believes, could greatly enhance the success rate of such endeavors.[40]

Zimmer addressed the important question of the relationship between ancient Indian and Greek medicine in a lecture entitled "The Influence of Hindu Medicine on Greek Medicine" given before the New York Academy of Medicine in 1942. He pointed to similarities between Indian and Greek notions of the six tastes or flavors, but stated that in Greece they did not, as in India, form the basis of dietetics and pharmacology. On the theory of humors, in India there were originally three, but in the medical classics of Caraka and Sushruta blood was added as a fourth. Since blood was a principal humor in Greek medicine, Zimmer argued that the occurrence of it in the Indian medical treatises could point to Greek influence. Nevertheless, he maintained that the basic conceptions of the Indian and Greek theories of humors were fundamentally different. Moreover, unlike the Greeks the Indians did not recognize diseases of the brain, for, as we have noted, the brain was unknown to the Indian physician. The many discrepancies between the two medical systems led Zimmer to the conclusion that on the whole they represented an "independent parallel growth and development. . . . While similarities cannot be denied," he

[38] Ibid., lvii.

[39] Francis Zimmermann, *The Jungle and the Aroma of Meats: An Ecological Theme in Hindu Medicine* (Berkeley and Los Angeles: University of California Press, 1987). See also Francis Zimmermann, *La discours des remèdes au pays des épices* (Paris: Editions Payot, 1989).

[40] Johannes Laping, "Dialogue in Research on Traditional Indian Medicine," in *Studies on Indian Medical History*, ed. D. Wujastyk and G. J. Meulenbeld (Groningen: Egbert Forsten, 1987), 239–41. An example of the kind of results obtained by combining areas of specialized knowledge to examine Indian materia medica is R. P. Labadie and K. T. D. de Silva, "*Centella asiatica* (L.); Urban in Perspective: an Evaluative Account," in the same volume, 207–23.

continues, "the more archaic system of the Hindus apparently was incapable of influencing Greek medicine and, in turn, remained outside the impact and spread of the Hellenistic achievements."[41]

But the book has yet to be closed on the fascinating and perplexing problem of possible influence between the two ancient traditions of medicine: it is an issue still being debated by scholars of both medical traditions. Addressing this same question, Francis Zimmermann has recently discovered several ideological similarities between the humors of ancient Greek and Indian medicine.[42] Likewise, G. Jan Meulenbeld, proceeding along the same lines as Zimmer, has noticed that in Ayurvedic veterinary texts blood is regarded as one of a set of four humors, and that in the classical Indian medical treatises blood is often described in terms very similar to those of a *dosha*. He speculates that a nosology based on four humors is very old in Indian medicine but that, over time, adaptations and changes reduced the number of humors to the standard three.[43]

Zimmer expresses his tentative conclusions about ancient Indian medicine in terms of a comparison with the Western medical tradition. He points out that Indian medicine never underwent the same transition to the critical scientific approach of the West because it was locked into the introspective system of inner experience and was inclined to consider subsidiary the range of empirical facts from the outer world. Hindu medicine is therefore characterized by conservatism and speculation based on intuition. "The deceptive satisfaction which this attitude of Hindu medicine afforded its adepts through its logical consistency and through the harmony of numbers, through the balance of characteristics, and through corresponding patterns, gave the Hindu doctor the illusion of real insight into the hidden connection and causations of facts, a glimpse, as it were, into the working of nature."[44] The Hindu medical insights were based, Zimmer claims, on a uniquely intuitive genius and actual command of the details of the Indian environment.

The apologetics implicit in Zimmer's concluding remarks conceal rather than reveal the specifically Indian medical perspectives he so

[41] *Hindu Medicine*, xlviii, li.

[42] Zimmermann, *La discours des remèdes au pays des épices*, esp. pp. 151–87.

[43] G. Jan Meulenbeld, "The Constraints of Theory in the Evolution of Nosological Classifications: A Study on The Position of Blood in Indian Medicine (Āyurveda)," in *Medical Literature from India, Sri Lanka and Tibet*, ed. G. Jan Meulenbeld (Leiden: E. J. Brill, 1991), 91–106, and "Conformities and Divergences of Basic Āyurveda Concepts in Veterinary Texts," *Journal of the European Āyurvedic Society* 1 (1991): 1–6.

[44] *Hindu Medicine*, 183.

skillfully elucidated in *Hindu Medicine*.[45] Although on closer scrutiny, Zimmer's interpretations are open to criticism, they are consistent with his understanding of ancient Indian thought. They derive from a life-time quest for an understanding of archaic man and thus cannot be dismissed as the musings of an eccentric German intellectual. Indeed, we are left to wonder how much deeper our knowledge of ancient Indian medicine would have been had Heinrich Zimmer lived to culti-vate the seeds of these early formulations.

Generally discounted by modern students of traditional Indian medicine for its eclecticism, Zimmer's study of Indian medical lore has been given scant attention. His solid training in the German tradition of Indology, however, provided him with the necessary tools to pene-trate to the core of this literature, and his broad interest in European intellectual history and world mythology gave him a wider perspec-tive from which to interpret its various layers. In addition, his admi-ration of Jung's analysis of the deep structures of the human mind and the role mythology played in understanding the unconscious led him to posit interpretations which hitherto had never been attempted. Es-pecially in light of recent trends in the study of ancient Indian medical lore, his scholarship deserves reexamination, even though he may not always have been completely correct. Careful examination of his analysis of Indian medical texts can, for example, provide data helpful in understanding the dynamics of important intellectual shifts in the tradition. This is true even though the crucial change from a purely "religious" to a fundamentally "scientific" conceptualization of the human body and the medical arts—the former dominating in the *Rig-veda* and *Atharvaveda*, the latter finding its first articulation in the med-ical compilations of Caraka and Sushruta—passed unnoticed by Zim-mer's otherwise discerning eye.

As Zimmer's study makes clear, the basic association between the microcosm and macrocosm prevalent in the early Vedic era provided an element of conservatism to the developing scientific mode of thought expressed in the early medical texts, but, perhaps as early as the anti-Brahmanical reflections of wandering ascetics, a radically new framework of understanding based largely in empiricism began rap-idly to supersede the mythological and sacrificial ideology of the Vedas. This intellectual shift might well indicate a radical change in the way the world was perceived. Time-honored Vedic paradigms could not accommodate new knowledge gained by close observation

---

[45] Edelstein reports that Zimmer regretted using the comparative approach to indicate what was unique in Indian medicine, for it severely diminished the significance of In-dian medical developments against what he perceived to be the acknowledged superior achievements of Western medical science.

of natural phenomena. Modifications were required, and to a great extent the early medical treatises were among the first repositories of these new intellectual developments. As Zimmer's study indicates, Hinduism is reluctant to abandon old modes of cognition for innovative ways of thinking, and the medical textbooks reflect the tension between conservatism and liberalism in medical thought. When new conceptualizations proved inadequate for certain types of empirical data, conservative ideas persisted, albeit often influenced by yoga-based intuition rather than doctrinal authority. The shifting sands of Brahminical thinking inspired by Upanishadic ascetics provided an opportunity to explore fresh approaches for explaining humankind and the surrounding world to which it was inextricably connected. To a large extent, then, the ancient Indian medical treatises are testaments to a transitional period in Indian intellectual evolution.[46]

[46] For a full discussion of the shift of the medical paradigm in ancient India, see Zysk, *Asceticism and Healing*.

8

SCHOPENHAUER'S *SHAKTI*

Matthew Kapstein

THE REFLECTIONS that follow are offered in response to the suggestion of my friend and colleague John Hawley, who, as organizer of the Zimmer centenary colloquium at Columbia University, asked that I provide an assessment of Heinrich Zimmer's contribution to the study of Indian philosophy. To do so is something of a challenge, for Zimmer's is not a name often invoked in connection with the contemporary study of Indian philosophy. And for good reason. Zimmer was no philosopher, and never identified himself as one. Nonetheless, his book *Philosophies of India* has enjoyed long popularity and, in the public imagination at least, has caused Zimmer's name to be widely associated with Indian philosophy, much as Will Durant's *The Story of Philosophy* created, in an earlier generation, a reputation for Durant as a philosophical publicist.[1] While there are aspects of Zimmer's work on Indian art and Tantrism that I think do command some philosophical interest, we should be clear at the outset about the decidedly nonphilosophical orientation of Zimmer's scholarship and the particular standpoint he adopted with respect to philosophy. For only when we have comprehended Zimmer's deliberate disaffinity with much of academic philosophy can we attempt to locate the genuine contributions to the philosophical study of classical India that may still be derived from his work.

In calling Zimmer's approach "nonphilosophical" I have in mind first and foremost his absolute disregard for what many contemporary philosophers would hold to be the indispensable features of philosophical method: rigorous definition and systematic argument, together with an insistence on well-crafted logical form as the appropri-

---

[1] Heinrich Zimmer, *Philosophies of India*, ed. Joseph Campbell, Bollingen Series XXVI (Princeton: Princeton University Press, 1969; originally published by the Bollingen Foundation in 1951). Like Zimmer, Durant also started out as a Schopenhauerian. I do not wish to suggest, however, that there were deep similarities between the two: Zimmer's vision of the transformative value of Indian spirituality is essentially at odds with Durant's insistence that "the story of civilization" is in most respects a Western tale.

ate vehicle for the elucidation of philosophical content. The immensity of Zimmer's disinterest here becomes apparent when we note that, with the exception of an appendix added by Joseph Campbell,[2] *Philosophies of India* makes not even perfunctory reference to the development of philosophical method in India, nor to the Nyaya and Vaisheshika schools and their Buddhist and Jaina counterparts, which represent (from a contemporary philosophical perspective, at least) the most characteristically *philosophical* aspects of classical Indian thought. Nor do Zimmer's earlier writings in German make up for this striking omission from his American lectures.[3] A comment from perhaps the most influential of recent authorities on Indian philosophy, the late Bimal K. Matilal, underscores the significance of such an omission for current investigations of Indian philosophy:

> A considerable portion of Indian philosophy consists of a number of rigorous systems which are more concerned with logic and epistemology than they are with transcendent states of euphoria. Verifications and rational procedures are as much as essential part of Indian philosophical thinking as they are in Western philosophical thinking. Thus, neglect of the study of Indian philosophy in modern philosophical circles is obviously self-perpetuating, for no one but the analytical philosophers will ever be able to recognize and make known in Western languages the counterpart to their own discipline.[4]

Which is to say, simply, that Indologists are generally confused about the nature of philosophy, while philosophers can't read Sanskrit. De-

---

[2] *Philosophies of India*, 605–14. One of the questions that arose during our discussions at the Southern Asian Institute colloquium on Zimmer concerned just how intrusive an editor Campbell had been. In the case of *Philosophies of India*, I believe that Campbell's "Editor's Foreword" (pp. v–vii) can be regarded as a substantially reliable guide to his admirably restrained editorial contribution. This conclusion is supported by the comparison of *Philosophies* with those among Zimmer's German works that offer the clearest precedents for it, chiefly *Indische Sphären*, 2d ed., in *Gesammelte Werke*, vol. 5 (Zurich: Rascher, 1963). See also the descriptions of the lecture courses from which *Philosophies* was derived—"Indo-Iranian" (u126) and "Indian Philosophy" (u128)—listed in the *Columbia University Bulletin of Information*, Forty-first Series, no. 35 (August 9, 1941), p. 129, and Forty-second Series, no. 31 (July 11, 1942). What we find here is a course outline essentially similar to the plan of *Philosophies* and similarly omitting any reference to the traditions of Indian logic. I am grateful to John Hawley for having taken the trouble to locate these artifacts of semesters long past.

[3] The best bibliographical survey is the "Selected Bibliography of Zimmer's Works" on pp. 261–67 of Heinrich Zimmer, *Artistic Form and Yoga in the Sacred Images of India*, trans. Gerald Chapple and James B. Lawson in collaboration with J. Michael McKnight (Princeton: Princeton University Press, 1984).

[4] Bimal K. Matilal, *Epistemology, Logic, and Grammar in Indian Philosophical Analysis* (The Hague and Paris: Mouton, 1971), 11–12.

spite this, some Indologists of Zimmer's generation, and some even earlier, had already made sufficient contributions to the uncovering of India's past traditions in logic and philosophical argument so that, had Zimmer been really interested in this material, he might readily have found substantial resources at his disposal.[5]

Shall we conclude, then, that Zimmer merely used the term *philosophy* in the casual manner that nonphilosophers are wont to do, being either ignorant of or willfully ignoring the concerns of those who regard philosophy as their proper domain? Perhaps Zimmer thought of philosophy in the way that I did when, as a nineteen-year-old student (who had read Zimmer), I arrived in India for the first time and was delighted to discover that everyone I met—the *rickshawala*, the *panwala*, the *dhobi*, no less than the *sadhu* or the *pandit*—was *a philosopher*. What I meant then was that everyone I spoke with seemed ready and able to express a complete worldview that was regarded as a fully coherent explanation of everything: "This whole world is the gift of Maheshvara," "Brahman is everywhere, in every creature," "No one escapes the fruit of karma," or what have you. It is not my intention now to disparage these and similar adages, or those who pronounce them: such affirmations might serve as either the conclusions of or the points of departure for philosophical reflection. But they do not of themselves constitute philosophical reflection. Philosophy happens when we ask just what is explained and how exactly the account that is offered serves to explain it, and whether the explanation is as coherent as its proponent affirms it to be.

Zimmer, to be sure, was not primarily interested in one-line affirmations either. He was concerned with the delineation of worldviews, rather than with the rational arguments advanced in connection with those worldviews. And he was profoundly concerned with the possibilities for human transformation disclosed in connection with the great worldviews of ancient India. Between Zimmer the philosopher and the philosophical *panwala*, then, the difference lies at least partially in the degree to which they elaborate their accounts, and the eloquence with which they do so. Some would certainly hold, and with some justification, that Zimmer's *Philosophies of India* comes close to exemplifying what Matilal had in mind when he wrote that:

---

[5] This is not the place to offer a bibliographical review of nineteenth- and early-twentieth-century investigations of Indian logic and related matters. Among those whose works Zimmer should have encountered at one point or another, we might mention E. B. Cowell, Surendranath Dasgupta, B. Faddegon, Ganganatha Jha, Hermann Jacobi, A. B. Keith, H. N. Randle, Stanislaus Schayer, Theodore Stcherbatsky, and Giuseppe Tucci.

The mass of publications which purport to be about "Indian philosophy," generally written by people who are totally unqualified in the discipline and which earns the boredom and annoyance of the professional philosopher, requires a little further comment: "Indian philosophy" has unfortunately come to denote a group of occult religious cults, a system of dogmas, and an odd assortment of spirituality, mysticism, and imprecise thinking, concerned almost exclusively with "spiritual liberation." Books, pamphlets, and other materials dealing with this theme are quite considerable in number and unfortunately too easily available.[6]

For, indeed, as if to illustrate the problem Zimmer himself writes:

> Our academic secular philosophies are concerned rather with information than with that redemptive transformation which our souls require. And this is the reason why a glance at the face of India may assist us to discover and recover something of ourselves.[7]

To the view that Zimmer the philosopher was really a genial non-philosopher dabbling in a field about which he was largely ignorant, however, there is one important objection: Zimmer in fact knew quite a lot of philosophy. A philosophical layman to be sure, he was nevertheless broadly conversant with the Western philosophical tradition and deeply knowledgeable about nineteenth-century German philosophy in particular, so that his relationship with academic philosophy must be regarded as a considered one, rather than as the product of sheer ignorance and misinformation. He was well aware of the tension between normative academic notions of philosophy and what he referred to as "Indian philosophy," a problem he introduces in *Philosophies of India* with these words:

> Many remained reluctant, even in the first years of the present century, to confer on Hindu thought the dignifying title "philosophy." "Philosophy," they claimed, was a Greek term, denoting something unique and particularly noble, which had sprung into existence among the Greeks and had been carried on only by Western civilization. To support this contention, they could refer to the authority of the giant Hegel, who, a full century before them . . . had discussed India and China in his *Philosophy of Religion* and *Philosophy of History*. . . . Hegel's argument—and it is still the argument of those who entertain the old reluctance to confer the title "philosopher" upon the immortal thinkers of India and China—is that something is missing from the Oriental systems. When they are compared

---

[6] Matilal, *Epistemology, Logic, and Grammar*, 10.
[7] Zimmer, *Philosophies of India*, 14.

with Western philosophy, as developed in antiquity and in modern times, what is obviously lacking is the ever renewed, fructifying close contact with the progressive sciences—their improving critical methods and their increasingly secular, non-theological, practically antireligious, outlook on man and the world. This is enough, we are asked to agree, to justify the Western restriction of its classical term.

Here, it must be admitted, the Old Guard are quite correct.[8]

This is not entirely unobjectionable: one may point to the influence of increased mathematical and astronomical knowledge during the Hellenistic period on Indian cosmological speculation, or that of medicine on yogic physiological conceptions, or to the many relationships between Vedic ritual and the sciences to whose rise it contributed, notably geometry and linguistics. Nevertheless, despite such evidence as we do find in India of the mutual relationship between scientific thought and philosophical and religious speculation, it remains true that the sustained scientific orientation of much of Western philosophy, particularly after the Renaissance, when science and academic philosophy became increasingly allied in their opposition to church dogmatics, sets it in sharp contrast with much of the Indian tradition. When we recall, however, that profoundly nonscientific and even antiscientific movements have nonetheless continued to emerge under the aegis of modern Western philosophy, Zimmer's intention at last comes clear. In contrast to recent apologists for the technical dimensions of classical Indian thought, he is engaged in a polemical assault on scientism, the tendency of modern Western thought to eliminate from its purview all that cannot be reduced to modes of explanation derived from the natural sciences. Zimmer's insistence on "Indian philosophy" is precisely conceived so as to underscore difference. This fundamental standpoint is confirmed by many other passages:

Western philosophy has become the guardian angel of right (i.e., unprejudiced, critical) thinking. It has earned this position through its repeated contacts with, and unwavering loyalty to, the progressive methods of thought in the sciences. And it will support its champion even though the

---

[8] Ibid., 29–30. Cf. Martin Heidegger, *What is Philosophy?* trans. Willaim Kluback and Jean T. Wilde ([New York]: Twayne Publishers: 1958): "The name 'philosophy' summons us into the history of the Greek origin of philosophy" (35). Heidegger, however, is not concerned simply to denote "something unique and particularly noble," as were the Hegelians to whom both he and Zimmer are alluding. Heidegger's concern, rather, is to point to the profoundly problematic nature of the historical phenomenon called "philosophy," and in this he and Zimmer would have found themselves, to some extent at least, in agreement. See also my "The Trouble with Truth," *Journal of the Indian Council of Philosophical Research* 9, no. 2 (1992): 69–85.

end may be the destruction of all traditional values whatsoever, in society, religion, and philosophy.[9]

That Zimmer's distaste for the elevation above all else of scientific and technical virtuosity was a determining feature of his intellectual orientation generally is in fact confirmed by his own revealing autobiographical remarks. Recollecting his student days, he writes that:

> My teacher in Sanskrit, Heinrich Lueders, was an arch-craftsman in philology, in deciphering manuscripts, inscriptions, a skilled super-mechanic, one of the past masters of philological craft in the field of Indic studies. But he was not interested in Indian thought, a plain liberal citizen from the republic of Luebeck, anti-philosophic, indifferent to mysticism, and with a meager sense for artistic qualities and implications. I was brought up on a wholesome diet of stones instead of bread.[10]

And, a few pages later, again referring to Lüders, he adds: "When I awakened to my own capabilities, in 1924/5, in writing *Kunstform und Yoga im indischen Kultbild*, I simply swept him overboard."[11]

Zimmer's pairing of "anti-philosophic" and "indifferent to mysticism" here is particularly illuminating. For Zimmer, the favored philosophy was not primarily academic philosophy at all; it was, rather, what is sometimes now referred to as "transformative philosophy," namely, those movements in thought that have emphasized above all the capacity of humankind for liberating spiritual transformation. "Transformative philosophy" is concerned with the spiritual condition of the person as a whole and in this respect overlaps with the varied tendencies in nineteenth-century thought that have been called *Lebensphilosophie*, "philosophies of life." The philosophers whom Zimmer most admired—Schopenhauer, Nietzsche, Dilthey, Deussen—are among the foremost of the "life philosophers."

If we are to form a clear conception of the significant philosophical elements of Zimmer's thought, especially in relation to the philosophies of life, we would do better to turn from the college lecture series represented by *Philosophies of India* to the work in which, by Zimmer's own account, his personal approach to the study of ancient India first crystallized, *Artistic Form and Yoga in the Sacred Images of India*. This deeply personal monograph, though not a work of philosophy, is nonetheless remarkably suggestive from a philosophical perspective: the reflections on interpretation, aesthetics, and Tantric thought found

---

[9] Zimmer, *Philosophies of India*, 31.
[10] Zimmer, "Some Biographical Remarks about Henry R. Zimmer," in *Artistic Form and Yoga*, 247.
[11] Ibid., 249.

within it remain for the most part vital even today. Indeed, it is perhaps only now, given the recent interest among students of India in
interpretation theory and in Tantrism, that an appropriate readership
for Zimmer's masterwork has been created.

That Zimmer was familiar with Wilhelm Dilthey (1833–1911) is certain.[12] It is very difficult, however, to establish the direct impact of
Dilthey's thought on Zimmer, and so it is perhaps better to speak here
of some of those areas in which Zimmer's intellectual concerns seem to
have at least resonated with Dilthey's, leaving the question of direct
influence to one side. Seen in this manner, a Diltheyian dimension to
Zimmer's thought is apparent throughout *Artistic Form and Yoga in the
Sacred Images of India*, a book that is paradigmatically an essay in interpretation. Although Zimmer does not attempt to set out a systematic
theory of interpretation at any point, *Artistic Form and Yoga* provides
us with ample evidence regarding some of the key assumptions that
Zimmer made about hermeneutical practice.

Dilthey was one of the leading proponents of the life philosophies
in nineteenth-century Germany, whose characteristic orientation finds
its clearest expression in the concept of *Erlebnis*, "lived experience,"
which forms the ground for all acts of understanding and interpretation. It is this emphasis on *Erlebnis* that constitutes one of Dilthey's
greatest contributions to the phenomenology of Edmund Husserl
(1859–1938) and his successors, and that gives to Dilthey's own
thought an unmistakably phenomenological cast. In the same vein, it
is the lived experience of the work of art that provides Zimmer with
the point of departure for his interpretive investigations:

> The classical work of art directs its appeal to our eye, promising us a
> glimpse of the infinite if our gaze does but follow its mysterious, beckon-
> ing call; we still have to ask where the appeal of Indian sculpture is di-
> rected—it is certainly not directed to our inquisitive eye. For the Indian
> figures refuse to take notice of us or to make eye contact with us that,
> once established, might then guide our eye over their richness of forms.
> Classical art appeals to our eye and to our eye alone. Anyone brought
> under its spell is physically galvanized, transformed into pure sight. With
> Indian sculpture, we circle about in vague disquiet; it does not look at us,
> and in vain do we try to capture its gaze.[13]

The experience of the Western eye first encountering Indian sculpture is one of disquiet, which discloses that we do not yet know how

---

[12] See *Philosophies of India*, 28, 64.
[13] Zimmer, *Artistic Form and Yoga*, 11.

to see what ostensibly stands within our gaze. Moved by this same disconcerting experience, Zimmer asks what the Indian tradition itself tells us of its sacred images. He finds an answer in the artistic prescriptions of the Puranas and Tantras, the devotional and esoteric texts that had been almost systematically avoided by nineteenth-century Indologists, who saw in these works endless perversions of fantasy and moral corruption. For Zimmer, however, these puzzling documents provided the key permitting us to undertake a sympathetic and imaginative reconstruction of the Hindu ritual experience. We cannot emphasize too much that for Zimmer this reconstruction was inevitably an original act of intellectual interpretation, for he was disdainful of Western attempts to assimilate Eastern wisdom through any of the various forms of spiritualism or theosophy that emerged during the late nineteenth and early twentieth centuries. In Dilthey's terms, I think Zimmer would have said that it is impossible for us simply to shed the preunderstanding that is the inheritance of our Western classical background; it *must* be the point of departure for our encounter with Indian art and religion.

The imaginative reconstruction of the ritual practice reveals the art object to express the unfolding of an inner vision in which the divine discloses itself. As such, the art object at once reflects the lived experience of the visionary as well as the purely transcendental nature of divinity, which may unfold in an inner vision but can never be considered as an artificial construction thereof. Dilthey, concerned as he was with the interpretation of Western art, emphasized that the art object was an expression of lived experience but seems to have placed less stress on its transcendental character.

The ritual function of the sacred image relates it immediately to functionally similar objects, and so, Zimmer insists, it should be studied together with the other sorts of schematic disclosures of the divine order, especially the Buddhist *mandalas* and Hindu linear *yantras*, that had frequently been categorized in the West quite separately from artworks.[14] By arguing that sacred image, ritual manual, and *yantra* dia-

---

[14] Zimmer's treatment of esoteric Buddhism generally leaves much to be desired: like other scholars of his generation he simply assumed that later Indian Buddhism dissolved back into Hinduism, almost completely losing its own identity in the process. Despite this, Zimmer's remarks on esoteric Buddhism do show frequent flashes of insight that speak miles for his interpretive genius and independence of thought. One small but telling example: his recognition of the significance of Avalokiteshvara's mantra—Om manipadme hum—against the long-held (and unfortunately still current) canard that this means "Hail to the Jewel in the Lotus!" (*Artistic Form and Yoga*, 204.) The comparative analysis of Tantric mantras and the Tibetan Buddhist commentarial tradition both support Zimmer's contention that *manipadme* is a feminine compound in the vocative case, meaning "O holder of the jewel and lotus!"—which are, indeed, the attri-

gram stand in a clear relationship both to one another and to the transforming inner vision that is mediated through them, however, Zimmer
was not merely reshuffling a deck stacked with cards drawn at random. His concern was that we enter into an understanding of a part of
the Indian experience of the sacred by endeavoring to comprehend the
whole. In this his strategy reflects Dilthey's difficult conception of the
role of the part-whole relationship in the interpretive act: only our understanding of the whole can disclose the significance of the part, and
only our grasp of the part can inform our understanding of the whole.
Understanding (*Verstehen*) irreducibly involves this circularlity.

Finally, we must add that Zimmer's approach to interpretation, like
Dilthey's, seems markedly positivistic when judged from a contemporary perspective: we may aspire, in Zimmer's world, to something ap-
proximating "correct" understanding, as he suggests by referring, for
instance, to "the true essence of Indian art." Likewise, interpretation,
for Dilthey, should arrive at something rather like objective truth. It
has recently been fashionable to castigate such a view as being very
obviously wrong. Against the fashionable assumption of the times,
which in certain of its cruder expressions seems to be obviously self-
refuting, the better corrective to the residual positivism of a Dilthey
or a Zimmer is to maintain that although "correctness" of interpretation is seldom, if ever, uniquely determined, this still leaves room
for determinations of incorrect interpretation: *mis*understanding is an
ever-present possibility.[15] We may therefore reject Zimmer's tendency
to adopt positivistic diction, while preserving much of his general
orientation.

Because Zimmer's experiment in the interpretation of Indian sacred
art is dependent throughout on his study of Tantrism, it will be useful
to consider in this context some of the distinctive features of his contribution to that obscure and difficult field.

The Western philosopher in whose work Zimmer seems to have sustained the deepest genuine interest was Arthur Schopenhauer (1788–
1860). Schopenhauer's peregrinations in Indian thought, and in the
Upanishads above all, are well known, as are his famous comparisons
of his own doctrines of the world as representation to the Vedantic

---

butes held by Avalokiteshvara. The "jewel in the lotus" error appears to originate only
in late-nineteenth-century British scholarship.

[15] For a very simple example, see the preceding note. This example nicely illustrates,
however, the manner in which some misinterpretations do take on a life of their own,
becoming virtually unquestioned in the process. Much of the study of Tantrism in fact
seems to be characterized by established misunderstandings in just this way.

notion of the veil of *maya* and of the extinction of the will to the Buddhist conception of *nirvana*. Less well known, at least among English-speaking philosophers, is the remarkable impact of Schopenhauer's thought on the study of Indian thought and culture during the late nineteenth and early twentieth centuries, particularly in Germany. The Indologist and historian of philosophy Paul Deussen may be counted chief among the heirs to Schopenhauer's legacy here, and as we thumb through the pages of the *Jahrbuch der Schopenhauer-Gesellschaft*, we discover that Indological contributions are found there in remarkable numbers. Small wonder, then, that an early-twentieth-century German Indologist, particularly one who was inclined to emphasize the primacy of lived experience, should have shown more than casual interest in Schopenhauer.

Zimmer, however, in fact showed much more than casual interest in Schopenhauer, enjoying something of a reputation as a Schopenhauer scholar in his own right. He contributed, for example, the standard biographical summary of Schopenhauer to *Die Grossen Deutschen: Deutsche Biographie*.[16] Nevertheless, his articles on Schopenhauer are really no more philosophical (at least in the "strict and technical" sense) than are his Indological writings and may be best considered as contributions to the history of ideas.

Although Schopenhauer felt that he had identified several important affinities between his own philosophy and classical Indian thought, one issue that long perplexed him was the relationship between his concept of the will and its possible Indian antecedents.[17] For some time he entertained the idea that the notion of *brahman*, the cosmic principle of a unity in which subject-object distinctions vanish, was itself the closest analogue. The will, for Schopenhauer, is the sole instance of what Kant had termed the "thing in itself" (*Ding an sich*), and in this respect it stands outside of all spatial and temporal determinations:

> The *will* as a thing in itself is quite different from its phenomenal appearance, and entirely free from all the forms of the phenomenal, into which it first passes when it manifests itself, and which therefore only concern its *objectivity*, and are foreign to the will itself. Even the most universal form of all ideas, that of being an object to a subject, does not concern it; still less the forms which are subordinate to this and which collectively

[16] Heinrich Zimmer, "Arthur Schopenhauer, 1788–1869," in Willy Andreas and Wilhelm von Scholz, eds., *Die Grossen Deutschen: Deutsche Biographie* (Berlin: Ullstein, 1936), 3:236–51; 2d ed., revised by Kurt Rossmann (Berlin: Ullstein, 1956), 3:134–51.
[17] The best survey to date of Schopenhauer's relation with Indian thought, as understood in Europe during his lifetime, will be found in Wilhelm Halbfass, *India and Europe: An Essay in Understanding* (Albany: State University of New York Press, 1988), 105–20.

have their common expression in the principle of sufficient reason, to which we know that time and space belong, and consequently multiplicity also, which exists and is possible only through these.[18]

The will as thing in itself, then, is free from all the characteristics of phenomenal existence, even one so apparently primary as the distinction of subject and object. Objectively, however, the will determines our experience in all of its phenomenal aspects. In this respect, it is eminently knowable:

> The word *will*, which, like a magic spell, discloses to us the inmost being of everything in nature, is by no means an unknown quantity, something arrived at only by inference, but is fully and immediately comprehended, and is so familiar to us that we know and understand that will is far better than anything else whatever.[19]

This is so because whenever we reflect upon ourselves, we find that the will proclaims its presence in our desires, motivations, inclinations, and so forth, of whatever kind. Our introspective knowledge of the nature of the will and of the ultimacy of its dictates permits us to detect its handiwork elsewhere as well:

> [Whoever] will recognize this will of which we are speaking not only in those phenomenal existences which exactly resemble his own, in men and animals as their inmost nature, but the course of reflection will lead him to recognize the force which germinates and vegetates in the plant, and indeed the force through which the crystal is formed, that by which the magnet turns to the north pole ... all these, I say, he will recognize as different only in their phenomenal existence, but in their inner nature as identical, as that which is directly known to him so intimately and so much better than anything else, and which in its most distinct manifestation is called *will*. ... It is the inmost nature, the kernel of every particular thing, and also of the whole. It appears in every blind force of nature and also in the preconsidered action of man; and the great difference between these two is merely in the degree of the manifestation, not in the nature of what manifests itself.[20]

Let us return now to Zimmer, whose vision of Tantric religion had as its focal point the notion of *shakti*, which he defines in these terms:

---

[18] Arthur Schopenhauer, *The World as Will and Idea*, trans. R. B. Haldane and J. Kemp (London: Kegan Paul, Trench, Trubner and Co., 1883), Book II, sec. 23. For an excellent recent assessment of Schopenhauer's doctrine of the will, and of his philosophy generally, see D. W. Hamlyn, *Schopenhauer* (London: Routledge and Kegan Paul, 1980).

[19] Schopenhauer, *The World as Will and Idea*, Book II, sec. 22.

[20] Ibid., sec. 21.

The central concept of tantric ideology is Śakti. Energy is held to be the essence of the world. Each personification of the Divine is seen as only one of the forms energy elects in order to make itself manifest. Eternal, divine Śakti divides itself into countless individual personifications of the Divine. But each divine personification, itself a manifestation of Śakti, develops Śakti further into a series of aspects that we may call its own *śaktis*. The idea of Śakti therefore frees the grand figures of the Hindu pantheon both from their autonomy as individuals and from their contentious rivalry with one another as a group, reducing them to the elemental concept they always had in common: to their very self, to divine energy. Śakti is the substance of the Divine; the diverse shapes it assumes are but apparitions—aspects of Śakti. The emergence of the idea of Śakti puts an end to a prolonged, ancient struggle for preeminence and sole authority among the separate ways we conceive of the Divine; no one of them emerges victorious from the conflict of sects and cults. Even though these ways vary in representing the richness of divine power and glory, they are of equal rank because each and every one, as a mere manifestation of the Divine, is subordinate to that idea ultimately constituting its divine nature: to Śakti, to divine energy.[21]

Further:

Within the several, duller levels of our consciousness of the phenomenal world's many differentiations, *śakti* realizes itself above all in the consciousness of the individual human soul, in *jīva*. But since nothing can exist apart from this divine spiritual energy, the lower worlds of animals and plants—even mountains and rocks—are simply stages of the unfolding of the one single Śakti into which, in play, it divided to form the duality of consciousness. Their lack of spirituality, their insensate nature exist only as opposites to the dimly lit spirituality of human consciousness; bound to this consciousness by its own *māyā*, the spiritual, that energy, does not know itself as the Universal One.[22]

It is primarily in his emphasis on "the Divine" that Zimmer's formulation departs notably from Schopenhauer's. Was Zimmer himself conscious that he had posited Schopenhauer's missing analogue? It is impossible to answer this with assurance on the basis of the passages cited above from *Artistic Form and Yoga*, but in a later article he himself underscored the connection: "Was Schopenhauer den 'Willen' nannte, heisst in Indien 'shakti', d.i. 'Kraft.'"[23]

---

[21] Zimmer, *Artistic Form and Yoga*, 153.

[22] Ibid., 25.

[23] "What Schopenhauer called 'Will' is called 'shakti' in India, that is to say, power" (Heinrich Zimmer, "Schopenhauer und Indien," *Jahrbuch der Schopenhauer-Gesellschaft* 25 [1938], 270). Generally speaking, Zimmer's understanding of *shakti*, as of Tantric thought

We should note, however, that Zimmer's conception of *shakti* departed from Schopenhauer's doctrine of the will in at least one very striking respect. Whereas Schopenhauer regarded *eros* to be the unadulterated expression of will, from whose painful grasp freedom was to be realized only by the extinction of the will in what he took to be nirvana, Zimmer saw the Tantras as overcoming the explicit dualism of any such formulation:

Everything in the world is Śiva and Śakti: in the sexual union of the spouses, the polar tension of the Divine's duality collapses into oneness; in this union, human consciousness crosses the borders of its isolation and enters a realm beyond polarities, to the point where it dissolves its polar nature—it becomes *nir-dvandva*. Eroticism in marriage is one means to the experiencing of one's own godlike nature, where the distinction between I and Thou disappears, where the world falls aways, where pain and desire and all the other polar opposites are transcended [*aufgehoben*].[24]

Zimmer was well aware of the persistent disparagement of the Tantras in European academic circles, the tendency to see within them only jumbled and incoherent fantasies said to be symptomatic of the corruption and degeneracy of later medieval Indian culture and religion. To his lasting credit as an interpreter of India, Zimmer recognized there to be much more to the story than that: the Tantras in fact embody a system, a distinctive way of thought, that succeeds in resolving many of the tensions inherent in earlier Indian thought and that informs Indian culture, especially its art and ritual, throughout. And in perceiving an affinity between the Hindu Tantric concept of *shakti* and Schopenhauer's *Wille*, Zimmer became perhaps the first Western thinker to suggest the possibility of comparative philosophical reflection with respect to the Tantras. One wonders, however, whether Zimmer's comparative insight could be profitably developed in an age to which Schopenhauer no longer speaks. Perhaps, then, it was for the best that in *Artistic Form and Yoga* that the connection was left unspoken.

Philosophies of India will continue to be widely read, for it is an entertaining, though dated and now about many matters unfashionable,

generally, was profoundly indebted to the work of Sir John Woodroffe (Arthur Avalon), a debt that Zimmer gratefully acknowledged, for example, in his autobiographical remarks in *Artistic Form and Yoga*, p. 254. Woodroffe even came close to a Schopenhauerian formulation in the title of his collection of essays, *The World as Power*, 3d ed. (Madras: Ganesh and Co., 1966), but, so far as I have been able to determine, never made this allusion explicit.

[24] Zimmer, *Artistic Form and Yoga*, 214.

118 MATTHEW KAPSTEIN

introduction to the world of ancient Indian religious thought.[25] To the study of Indian philosophy, however, Zimmer's enduring contribution is doubtlessly *Artistic Form and Yoga*. The peculiar questions that Zimmer raises there, and the peculiar approach he adopts in seeking to resolve them, merit the continuing consideration of students Indian art and esotericism, and equally the attention of the philosophers.

[25] One aspect of *Philosophies of India* strikes me as being profoundly problematic, however. This is Zimmer's much flaunted notion of an "Aryan-Dravidian synthesis." Zimmer seems to have harbored the view that was popular during the nineteenth century, and ironically made into a party dogma by the National Socialists, whom Zimmer detested, that different racial lines were rather strictly correlated with systems of belief. Thus, the history of ideas could be regarded as a story about the intermingling and dividing of human races. That Zimmer thought in these terms persistently, though perhaps without clearly thinking through the implications, may be seen in his autobiographical notes in *Artistic Form and Yoga*: "On her father's side [Zimmer's mother] was of German-Saxon extraction. . . . Her mother . . . was of Wendish stock. . . . This Saxon-Wendish stock is inclined to mysticism, as are kindred folk in Silesia. . . . This may account for my predilection for mysticism, myths and symbols, while the Pre-German, Pre-Celtic, Pre-Aryan descent of my father from the ancient European matriarchal civilization explains my penchant for the corresponding stratifications in ancient Pre-Aryan Hindu civilization (the Great Mother, the feminine principle in Tantrism)" (253). In fact, Zimmer probably inherited this nonsense directly from his father, also named Heinrich Zimmer (1851–1910), on whose own application of racialist theories to India, see Ronald Inden, *Imagining India* (Oxford: Basil Blackwell, 1990), 178.

9

ZIMMER AND COOMARASWAMY

VISIONS AND VISUALIZATIONS

Mary F. Linda

The *Art of Indian Asia* is accepted as Heinrich Zimmer's exegesis of the Buddhist and Hindu art of South and Southeast Asia. Edited by Joseph Campbell from lecture notes prepared by Zimmer at Columbia University in 1941 and from earlier notes, the text, with an accompanying volume of plates, was published in 1955, twelve years after Zimmer's death.[1] It was intended by the publishers to serve as an introduction to Indian art, rather than a chronological, historical account of its development. Zimmer would doubtless have approved of this intent, for none of his writings extensively address the relevance of chronology or the development of style and, in fact, his interests were interpretive rather than historical, whether he was expounding on textual or visual material. But one wonders if Zimmer would have appreciated the publication of this text, which in contrast to his earlier powerfully written and insightful publications was thematically fragmented, with some information out of date by the time of its publication, and which presented ideas uninformed by more recent art historical literature.

Reviews of the book in 1955 and 1956 by Stella Kramrisch, Benjamin Rowland, and LeRoy Davidson called attention to the strengths and weaknesses of Zimmer's thought in *The Art of Indian Asia*.[2] All three reviewers highly valued Zimmer's eloquent recital of myths and exuberant descriptions of feminine beauty (the archetypal mother goddess), which revealed a sensitive comprehension of Indian sculpture informed by a knowledge of the ritual and of the beliefs that determined its form. Regarding Zimmer's extensive discussion of the symbolism of the lotus (which Davidson also found most stimulating),

---

[1] Heinrich Zimmer, *The Art of Indian Asia*, 2 vols., ed. Joseph Campbell, Bollingen Series XXXIX (1955; 2d ed., rev., Princeton: Princeton University Press, 1968), v.

[2] Stella Kramrisch, "India: Unfinished Panorama," *Art News* 54, no. 5 (1955): 40, 50, 57–58; idem, *Artibus Asiae* 18, no. 3/4 (1955): 328–35; Benjamin Rowland, Jr., *College Art Journal* 15, no. 2 (1955): 167–69; J. LeRoy Davidson, *Art Bulletin* 38, no. 2 (1956): 124–27.

Kramrisch remarked: "Never before have myth and iconography been given deeper or fuller interpretation."[3] Kramrisch also acknowledged, and agreed with, Zimmer's hermeneutics of Puranic and Tantric thought: the theme of pairs of opposites (life and death, time and eternity, creation and destruction) that the enlightened devotee understands as one is woven throughout the book. With this insight, Zimmer had "stepped into Indian art to its core."[4] At the same time, "The quality of exhaltation expressed in his words, and aroused by the works of art, is not a direct response to their form; it is rather an association with contents, evoked by their appearance."[5] Indeed, for Zimmer, an image was a composite of symbols that were visualizations of eternal realities originally expressed in myths. His interest in Indian art was inspired primarily by his extensive study of Tantric texts; not until 1925 did Zimmer actually examine original sculptures in Paris, probably at the Musée Guimet.[6]

Perhaps because Zimmer's expertise was mythology, and sculpture only an extension of that interest, he failed to comprehend that a more ordered knowledge of the variety of art found throughout the subcontinent could have confirmed his conclusions (or not) and perhaps could have suggested nuances of interpretation. Essentially, in refusing seriously to acknowledge that the art he discussed was formally transformed over time and in different geographical regions, he left himself vulnerable to criticism. As Davidson succinctly stated: "The understanding of Indian art depends . . . on the knowledge of temporal and human forces, as well as on that of philosophic and religious texts. . . . Any introduction to Indian art which ignores the transmutation of ideas by man and time presents only a partial and romanticized picture, no matter how many philosophic refinements it may incorporate."[7]

The chapters on architecture, moreover, lack the insight and lyrical descriptions of the chapters on sculpture. If mythology was of primary interest to Zimmer and sculpture secondary, architecture was definitely tertiary. He never saw a Hindu temple in its physical or cultural situation and, perhaps as a result, developed less enthusiasm for, and understanding of, architecture than sculpture, which he could see in

[3] Kramrisch, *Art News*, 57.

[4] Kramrisch, *Artibus Asiae*, 329.

[5] Ibid.

[6] Heinrich Zimmer, "Some Biographical Remarks about Henry R. Zimmer," appendix in *Artistic Form and Yoga in the Sacred Images of India*, trans. Gerald Chapple and James B. Lawson in collaboration with J. Michael McKnight (Princeton: Princeton University Press, 1984), 255. Originally published as *Kunstform und Yoga im indischen Kultbild* (Berlin: Verlags-Ansalt, 1926).

[7] Davidson, *Art Bulletin*, 126.

European museums. One original idea he put forward—that the wood and thatch Toda huts of South India were the basis for rock-cut caves such as Lomas Rishi in North India—was dismissed outright as meaningless by Davidson.[8] Indeed, Zimmer gives no indication, here or elsewhere, of having read Coomaraswamy's article on early Indian architecture as depicted in reliefs, which contains an extensive discussion of the relationship of wooden to stone architecture.[9]

Truth be told, little factual information and few original ideas were presented in *The Art of Indian Asia*. Whatever "facts" were included—as opposed to the interpretations that are woven through the text—must have been culled by Zimmer from published archaeological reports and previously published analyses of Indian art. For example, the identifications and descriptions of the *jataka* stories on the *toranas* (gateways) of Sanchi Stupa I had been taken almost verbatim from Ludwig Bachhofer's *Early Indian Sculpture*.[10] In fairness to Zimmer, though, it must be reiterated that it is by no means clear he intended his lecture notes to be published, and what was published was prepared by someone other than himself.

The question of authorship of *The Art of Indian Asia* therefore becomes relevant. To what extent were Zimmer's ideas, along with his notes, reorganized and edited by Campbell? Moreover, other people may have had an impact on the final text. Ananda K. Coomaraswamy, one of the most prominent art historians of Indian art in the first half of this century, was curator at the Boston Museum of Fine Arts from 1917 to 1947. His *History of Indian and Indonesian Art* (1927), the only survey book on the subject available at the time, was the textbook Zimmer used for his class at Columbia. Campbell consulted Coomaraswamy while he was editing *Myths and Symbols in Indian Art* (1946) and referred to Coomaraswamy's text when compiling *The Art of Indian Asia*. Is it possible that, in addition to whatever direct influence Coomaraswamy may have had on Zimmer, Campbell also integrated certain of Coomaraswamy's ideas into Zimmer's notes? Indeed quite apart from the fact that the scope of the two texts is similar, the arrangement of the sections on Hindu architecture in *The Art of Indian Asia* is comparable to that in Coomaraswamy's earlier work.

A detailed attempt to discern "who contributed what" to the final text of *The Art of Indian Asia*, however, would probably prove fruit-

---

[8] Heinrich Zimmer, "Trees, Huts and Temples," trans. Stella Kramrisch, *Journal of the Indian Society of Oriental Art* 5 (1937): 111–21; Davidson, *Art Bulletin*, 127.

[9] Ananda K. Coomaraswamy, "Bodhigharas, Palaces," *Eastern Art* 3 (1931): 181–217.

[10] Ludwig Bachhofer, *Early Indian Sculpture* (Paris: Pegasus Press, 1929). Compare the descriptions in the list of plates for the Sanci great *stupa* (pp. xxiii–xxvi) and the Saddanta Jataka on p. 41 with Zimmer, *Art of Indian Asia*, pp. 238–44.

less—and runs the risk of diverting attention from the originality and power of Zimmer's thinking in his earlier publications. Actually, Zimmer's earlier publications record more faithfully and coherently his ideas that have had an impact on our understanding of Indian art. Other lines of inquiry are therefore more intriguing. What ideational constructs prevalent in Germany influenced Zimmer's intellectual development, and what personal characteristics compelled his research interests? Once Zimmer became interested in art, what textual and human sources shaped his ideas? Did Coomaraswamy in fact influence Zimmer's thinking? Another prolific and prominent writer on Indian art and its symbolism during Zimmer's lifetime was Stella Kramrisch. How influential were her ideas?

That the three knew or knew of one another, at least to some degree, and recognized a commonality of intellectual approach to Indian art is clear. Zimmer reviewed Kramrisch's translation of one of the Puranas, the *Vishnudharmottara*, in 1926 and her *Grundzüge der indischen Kunst* (Fundamentals of Indian Art) in 1927.[11] Sometime after this, Kramrisch and Zimmer probably met on a train from London to Oxford. Although she felt that his lack of personal experience of India made his opinions overly subjective, she admired his work enough to translate two of his articles into English and arrange for their publication in the *Journal of the Indian Society of Oriental Art*.[12]

Coomaraswamy praised Zimmer's *Kunstform und Yoga* in a 1932 review, in which he stated that "no more valuable book for the understanding of Indian art . . . has yet been published."[13] Coomaraswamy thought Zimmer to "be the ideal scholar, at the same time erudite and creative, able to gather material rigorously but also able to see its significance."[14] Coomaraswamy's sustained admiration for Zimmer's thought is further revealed in a review of Zimmer's posthumously published *Myths and Symbols in Indian Art*.[15] The appreciation seems to have been mutual. In an undated letter to Coomaraswamy, Zimmer stated: "I need not say how much it means to me to have met you personally. Your inspiring way of dealing with Hindu

---

[11] Heinrich Zimmer, *Artibus Asiae* 1, no. 3 (1925–1926): 236–37; *Orientalistische Literaturzeitung* 30, no. 3 (March 1927): 191–94.

[12] The meeting of Kramrisch and Zimmer is mentioned in the biographical essay in Barbara Stoler Miller, ed., *Exploring India's Sacred Past: Selected Writings of Stella Kramrisch* (Philadelphia: University of Pennsylvania Press, 1983), 18. Zimmer's articles translated by Kramrisch were "Some Aspects of Time in Indian Art," *Journal of the Indian Society of Oriental Art* 1, no. 1 (1933): 30–51; and "Trees, Huts and Temples."

[13] Ananda K. Coomaraswamy, *Artibus Asiae* 4, no. 1 (1930–32): 78–79.

[14] Roger Lipsey, ed., *Coomaraswamy*, 3 vols., Bollingen Series LXXXIX (Princeton: Princeton University Press, 1977), vol. 3, *His Life and Work*, by Roger Lipsey, p. 212.

[15] Ananda K. Coomaraswamy, *Review of Religion* 11, no. 3 (March 1947): 285–91.

art and religion has, since I became a student, been one of the main elements of my initiation into this revelation of truth."[16]

Coomaraswamy and Kramrisch were also acquainted. He reviewed a revised and enlarged edition of Kramrisch's translation of the *Vishnudharmottara* in 1932 and her *Indian Sculpture* in 1934, which he regarded as "the best existing introduction to the subject within its chosen limits."[17] In a 1947 article on the symbolism of the Hindu temple, he referred to her recently published book *The Hindu Temple* (1946) as a magnificent work.[18] On her part, Kramrisch apparently had the highest regard for Coomaraswamy's intellectual seriousness and dedicated the 1937 issue of the *Journal of the Indian Society of Oriental Art* to him on his sixtieth birthday.[19]

The work of all three could be characterized in general as more interpretive than descriptive. Each recognized the transcendental and therefore symbolic nature of Indian art—Indian art was a mirror of a real world that was intangible—and therefore each sought to understand iconology, the meaning behind the forms. And, in contrast to previous scholars, each extensively consulted various types of texts to interpret this iconology. Kramrisch, who spent thirty years in India, had greater firsthand knowledge particularly of temples, but also of sculpture, than either Coomaraswamy or Zimmer. Probably because of this, she focused more in her earlier writings on the chronology and development of forms. Her metaphysical observations, which were not extensively presented until her monumental publication on the symbolism of the Hindu temple in 1946, four years after Zimmer's death, were less prominent in this early scholarship. It is not surprising then, that there are no clear indications in Zimmer's writings on art that he was influenced deeply by Kramrisch's thoughts.

His interests in metaphysics and aesthetics more closely corresponded to Coomaraswamy's interests. It would be more fruitful, then, especially given Zimmer's acknowledgment of Coomaraswamy as inspirational for him, to examine the work and possible intellectual interaction of these two. Zimmer's single most important interpretive work on Indian aesthetics was *Kunstform und Yoga*, published in 1926, on which I will rely almost exclusively. Coomaraswamy's theoretical writings extended throughout his lifetime, and I will focus on these to

[16] Lipsey, ed., *Coomaraswamy*, 3:212.

[17] Ananda K. Coomaraswamy, *Journal of the American Oriental Society* 52, no. 1 (1932): 13–21 and ibid. 54, no. 2 (1934): 219.

[18] Lipsey, ed., *Coomaraswamy*, vol 1, *Selected Papers, Traditional Art and Symbolism*, by A. K. Coomaraswamy, p. 3. See also Stella Kramrisch, *The Hindu Temple*, 2 vols. (Calcutta: University of Calcutta, 1946).

[19] Miller, *Exploring India's Sacred Past*, 27.

the exclusion of his art historical works.[20] Although each author wrote
in response to different personal and intellectual contexts, both were
reacting to the negative critiques of Indian art prevalent in Europe in
the early twentieth century, and they came to similar conclusions
about the nature of Indian art and aesthetics.

Ananda K. Coomaraswamy (1877–1947) was born in Sri Lanka to a
British mother and a Tamil Hindu father, who died when Coomaraswamy was two. Thereafter he was raised and educated in England as
a geologist and only returned to Sri Lanka in 1902, where he resided
for just five years.[21] Although Coomaraswamy intermittently traveled
to India, most of his life was spent in the West, but because of his background and consequent mission, he came to represent and defend the
East. His first major work, *Mediaeval Sinhalese Art*, published in 1908
upon his return to England, reflects knowledge of and involvement
with the contemporary debates in England about both the decadence
and needed reform of industrial design and about the nature of Indian
art. Notable in this debate were Sir George Birdwood and William
Morris, both of whom attributed the strength in conception and execution of Indian design to the fact that the designs were produced by a
living tradition within the traditional Indian village social structure.[22]
The idea that a traditional social structure had to lie behind design of
any real quality was used to oppose industrialism, which was blamed
for the decline in English—and, under British administration, Indian—
craftsmanship.

Taking an opposing point of view, John Ruskin added a moral twist
to the debate on the aesthetics of Indian art. Convinced of the cruelty
and immorality of Indians he concluded that, although Indian decorative designs were acceptable because their production need not in-
volve the intellect or a developed moral sense, Indian sculpture was
inferior in quality to European.[23] Inhuman and despotic people were
not capable of creating fine art, he said. His evaluation of Indian art
further turned on the issue of fidelity to nature, an important theme
in art criticism at the time. Direct imitation of nature was central to

[20] For a bibliography of Coomaraswamy's writings, see Lipsey, ed., *Coomaraswamy*,
3:293–304. The most extensive bibliography of Zimmer's works is in Zimmer, *Artistic
Form and Yoga*, 261–67.

[21] Lipsey, ed., *Coomaraswamy*, vol. 3, chaps. 1 and 2.

[22] Partha Mitter, *Much Maligned Monsters* (Oxford: Clarendon Press, 1977), 221–36.
Owen Jones and Sir George Birdwood most stringently decried the evils of Western industrialism.

[23] Ibid., 238–46. The works of Ruskin cited most often by Mitter are *Modern Painters*,
Lectures on Art, *Aratra Pentelici*, and *The Two Paths*.

Ruskin's theory of art, and since Indian art was abstract and symbolic, and lacked fidelity to nature, he considered it irrational.

Concurrent with the debate on the aesthetics of Indian art in the late nineteenth and early twentieth century were attempts to develop a history of Indian art that would both construct a chronological framework and allow for aesthetic evaluations. The cultural historian Partha Mitter has divided these scholars into two groups: the archeologists, who were primarily concerned with the sequential ordering of sculpture and architecture in time and place and who accepted the superiority of the classical Western style; and the transcendentalists, who rejected this assumed supremacy and sought to understand the aesthetics and symbolism of Indian art.[24]

The basic ideas of the archeologists were as follows. Indian architecture was a true style because its form was adequate to its function, but it was inferior to even imitative European architecture. Indian art was to be classified by religious and chronological categories (Buddhist, Hindu, and Islamic) or by region (Indo-Aryan north and Dravidian south). This art had evolved from simple to more complex forms, and Buddhist art was superior because of its simplicity. Subsequent Hindu art, with its many-armed and ferocious gods (long considered irrational in Europe), was, however, degenerative—the result of the reassertion of the indigenous Dravidian element. The superiority of European art and race was considered self-evident: Indian sculpture was evaluated by classical standards and, since it did not represent ideal types in nature, was found wanting. "Good" Indian art (the early Mauryan capitals, and the Buddhist art at Sanchi, Amaravati, and Gandhara) was derived from the Western classical tradition and/or executed by Greek artisans.

Publications by E. B. Havell and A. K. Coomaraswamy in the first decade of the twentieth century controverted many of these attitudes of the archaeologists.[25] Havell, the principal of the Calcutta School of

<hr/>

[24] Ibid., 253–86. A more detailed analysis of contributions made during this period to the history of Indian art may be found in Pramod Chandra, *On the Study of Indian Art* (New York: The Asia Society, 1983); the essay on architecture may also be found in idem, ed., *Studies in Indian Temple Architecture* (New Delhi: American Institute of Indian Studies, 1975), 1–40. Of the archeologists, Mitter discusses the work of Henry Cole and James Fergusson; Chandra discusses the work of these two and of Cunningham, Burgess, Jouveau-Dubreuil, Foucher, Marshall, and Stern. The transcendentalists that Mitter examines are Havell and Coomaraswamy, to which Chandra adds Kramrisch.

[25] E. B. Havell, *Indian Sculpture and Painting* (London: John Murray, 1908), and *The Ideals of Indian Art* (London: John Murray, 1911); Coomaraswamy, *Mediaeval Sinhalese Art* (1908; repr. New York: Pantheon, 1956), and *The Indian Craftsman* (London: Probsthain & Co., 1909). See also Pramod Chandra, ed., *The Art Heritage of India* (Bombay: D. B. Taraporevala Sons & Co. Private Ltd., 1964), pt. 1.

Art, objected to the frequent attribution of foreign influence and rejected the application of classical standards to Indian art, which he
thought must be evaluated by indigenous standards. In order to understand this art, he argued, it was necessary to comprehend the philosophical, religious, and mythological ideas embedded in it and, most
important, to comprehend the purpose of the artist. Indian art was
idealistic, mystical, and symbolic, a spiritual art that embodied a
transcendental ideal rather than "the appearance of objects (nature)
perceived by human senses. . . . Its main endeavor is always directed
towards the realization of an idea, reaching through the finite to the
infinite."[26] The artist, who gave form to the infinite, depended on a
spiritual vision to produce images of the gods. This spiritual vision
was acquired by meditation exercises (yoga), during which the artist's
identity merged with that of the invoked divinity.[27]

Given that Western standards were still the criteria for evaluation of
Indian art, biases persisted in England regarding the sculpture—the
"fine art"—of India. These views were given succinct expression by Sir
George Birdwood on the occasion of a 1910 lecture by Havell to members of the Royal Society of Arts.[28] According to Birdwood, who was
familiar with Havell's work and who had a deep appreciation of Indian applied arts, no "fine art" existed in India because there was no
art for art's sake. Rather, Indian art was utilitarian, a monstrous representation of a deity for ritual. Whereas Western art was inspired by the
artist's own ideals of the good, the beautiful, and the true, Indian art
was canonically prescribed, and only infrequently did this result in a
classical statue. More often, the result was a hideous image. Western
art had universal appeal, but an appreciation of Indian art could derive only from an understanding of its symbolism. Art was but the
framework, and as fine art no different from an algebraic formula. The
direct study of nature was the basis of Western art; the only reference
for the Indian artist was his inner vision achieved through meditation.

Birdwood's strong emotional and intellectual distaste for Indian art
was evident in his description of a Javanese seated Buddha sculpture,
which his audience would have understood to apply likewise to Indian sculpture generally:

[26] Havell, *Ideals of Indian Art*, 137.

[27] Ibid., 140. Havell relies on Foucher's reading of Buddhist texts in the Cambridge
University Library and in the Bibliothèque Nationale, Paris, for this information. See
A. Foucher, *Etude sur l'iconographie bouddhique de l'Inde* (Paris: Ernest Leroux, 1905), 1–14.

[28] E. B. Havell, "Arts Administration in India," *Journal of the Royal Society of Arts* 58
(February 1910): 273–98, which records the lecture by Havell. Sir George Birdwood introduced him and then commented on his critique of British arts administration, where-
upon Coomaraswamy responded to Birdwood.

This senseless similitude, in its immemorial fixed pose, is nothing more that an uninspired brazen image, vacuously squinting down its nose to its thumbs, and knees, and toes. A boiled suet pudding would serve equally well as a symbol of passionless purity and serenity of soul! It is in vain to argue that such imbecilities are objects of "fine art" because of the thoughts or emotions they excite in the devout.[29]

Responding to Birdwell, Coomaraswamy echoed many of Havell's ideas. But his remarks also foreshadowed his lifelong quest to understand and explain Indian art to a Western audience:

> The writer of books on art should aim to make his readers understand the art; to see the world as the artist saw it; at least to know what the artist wished to say. . . . The European critic never seemed to penetrate behind the surface of an Indian sculpture or painting, or to have learnt its language; he did not perceive its intention, and therefore, could not judge it on its own true basis.[30]

Every major theme that would preoccupy Coomaraswamy throughout his lifetime, either because of his political convictions or in response to the bombastic, denegrating European criticisms of Indian art, was stated in seminal form in his monumental study *Mediaeval Sinhalese Art* of 1908. Indeed, these ideas could almost be viewed as an outline that Coomaraswamy would flesh out in the years to come. His fundamental assumption was that traditional art and society were ideal, and that anything post-Renaissance was decadent and untrue. Coomaraswamy never accepted that the Industrial Revolution had changed the course of history and the structure of society; he consistently glorified the past, whose characteristics may have been to a considerable extent the product of his own imagination.[31]

According to Coomaraswamy, traditional society, such as that of precolonial Ceylon until the eighteenth century, was like that of pre-Renaissance, medieval Europe: non-materialistic, ordered, and coherent. Thus it produced the best and purest forms of art.[32] All artistic creation in a traditional society was an expression of a religious conception of life; religion and art were inseparable. This was "true" art because the forms expressed the divine, not some individualistic sentiment. The art was "ideal" in that it was inspired by an abstract idea

[29] Ibid., 287.

[30] Ibid., 290.

[31] Geoffrey Cook, "Ananda K. Coomaraswamy and Medieval Sri Lankan Art," *Left Curve*, no. 15 (1991): 76.

[32] This idea became so solidified in Coomaraswamy's mind that toward the end of his life he freely interchanged European and Indian sources and vocabularies when discussing Indian art.

rather than being an imitation of nature. Reality existed in the mind and was controlled by the divine architect Vishvakarma, who revealed it in dreams to the artist. For his part, the artist practiced yogic purification rituals and meditation in order to visualize the dream image; never was the artist to observe the object itself in nature. The artist was part of the universe, a repository of all artists, who had worked out the language of art long ago. Thus the artist did not strive for individual expression but gave substance to ideals of eternal beauty and unchanging laws. Artistic tradition, the divinely prescribed canons of proportion and iconography revealed in texts, was a support, not a hindrance, to the expression of great art.

Coomaraswamy's perspective was encyclopedic in scope, and he relied extensively on original religious and architectural texts to support and explicate his ideas about the art that he observed in these early years. Coomaraswamy's later work divides into two categories: metaphysics, aesthetics, and the theory of art on the one hand, and historical studies on the other. As Coomaraswamy grew older, theoretical issues increasingly occupied his interest, although because he was curator at the Boston Museum of Fine Art he continued intermittently to produce topical art historical studies. Moreover, despite Coomaraswamy's growing fascination with theory, it was the latter studies—his *History of Indian and Indonesian Art* and his monographs on the origin of the Buddha image, on architectural forms such as cities, gates, tree shrines, and palaces, on *yakshas*, on Buddhist iconography, and on the symbolism of the dome—that established his reputation as an art historian. But even in these studies the freshness of his approach came through. According to Pramod Chandra, Coomaraswamy "was responsible for reestablishing the study of Indian art, whether architecture, sculpture, or painting, on a new basis."[33] In contrast to earlier scholars, Coomaraswamy investigated beyond time and place (chronology and style), seeking to understand the inner meaning, or symbolism, of sculpture or architecture by combining observations of forms with reference to texts—two sources previously studied independently of each other.

Heinrich Zimmer developed in quite different personal and intellectual circumstances from Coomaraswamy. His father was professor of Celtic philology at the University of Berlin, as well as a Sanskrit scholar, and thus Zimmer was imbued from birth with the "great scholarly traditions characteristic of German learning."[34] He com-

---

[33] Chandra, *On the Study of Indian Art*, 31.
[34] David Friedman, "Obituary," *Review of Religion* 8, no. 1 (1943): 14–16.

pleted his Ph.D. in philology and comparative linguistics in 1914 at Berlin. Despite this strong academic background, he developed an essentially romantic image of India, one that was never informed by a visit there. In contrast to Coomaraswamy, who, as a South Asian, was confronted with extremely negative views of India and its "monstrous" art, Zimmer lived in an environment accepting of India—but of a mythic India.

German romanticism had created a myth of India that was based on the writing of Greek historians, as well as on travel literature and translations of a limited number of Sanskrit texts, much of it produced in response to a longing for the reunion of man and nature, for a revival of the unity perceived between art and religion in the Middle Ages, and for a quest for primal verities that would explain the common origin of religion, language, and art. For the German romantics in the second half of the eighteenth century, India was the place where culture first developed and was then transmitted to the ancient world; it was the source of all wisdom, religion, and language, a curious blend of the primitive (a preindustrial, "intuitive" society) and the sublime (arts, sciences, and philosophy).[35] The Hindu was an unspoiled child of nature, simple, gentle, intelligent, who lived a life of ease in an idyllic land of natural abundance. A superior class of holy men, Brahmans, guarded this civilization, and poetry (*kavya*) permeated every aspect of unified human wisdom. Johann Gottfried Herder (1744–1803), who formulated in his writings much of the mythic image, recognized that the Hindu god could not be perceived by the human senses and required primary symbols to depict his attributes, symbols that represented to the Hindu the principles of his religion.

Early in the nineteenth century, Friedrich Creuzer (1771–1858) made Indian myths and symbols in art the cornerstone of his *Symbolik und Mythologie der alten Volker* (1810).[36] Interested in the relationship between the classical world and India, Creuzer thought symbols signified a particular idea, that they were a sign language with mystical meaning, created by priests to teach moral truths—in short, visual guides to divinity. Symbols were the simplest and most archaic form of human expression; those of the Orient were enigmatic, mystical, and untranslatable; symbolic art expressed the profound ideas and the diverse relationships that existed in theology, and images in primitive societies were for meditation on the divine.

Creuzer's ideas were to have an impact on one of the most influen-

---

[35] See A. Leslie Willson, *A Mythical Image: The Ideal of India in German Romanticism* (Durham, N.C.: Duke University Press, 1964), esp. the foreword and introduction, and pp. 28–36 and 49–70.

[36] Mitter, *Much Maligned Monsters*, 203–7.

tial nineteenth-century thinkers on world art, Georg Wilhelm Friedrich Hegel (1770–1831).[37] Hegel, too, thought that art represented an
ideal world beyond the visual, objective one. In Hegel's view, symbolic
art was the first of three stages in the history of world art: symbolic (in
which there is a contradiction between form and meaning), classic
(representing a balance of form and meaning), and romantic (in which
spirit dominates over matter). Hegel also held that different traditions
represented different ideals that reflected a national spirit; to judge a
given nation's art, it was thus necessary to understand its ideals and to
what point in history that nation belonged. Because the Indian philosophic tradition denied individuality, India therefore lacked a factual,
true depiction of history. To Hegel, everything in India, the Hindu experience of life, happened as if in a dream. But, although Indian art
possessed a meaning beyond the directly perceptible, it was not a true
symbolic art: the potential to advance to the classic stage was nonexistent. Ultimately for Hegel, then, Indian art, although a spiritual art,
was static and irrational.

Zimmer's initial interest in India was stimulated by emotional reso-
nances more akin to the longings of the eighteenth-century romantics
than to the "scientific" approach of nineteenth-century scholars, although Zimmer was also concerned with some of the ideas that occupied the latter: myths, symbols, the transcendental nature of art, and
the unconscious. Disenchanted with the academic stagnation of German universities in the first decade of the twentieth century, Zimmer
perceived India, through Indian literature, in terms similar to those of
the romantics: as the ultimate source of civilization, a primitive place,
and yet one possessing transforming wisdom:

> I could not stand the stale and dull atmosphere of pseudoromantic West-
> ern medievalism. . . . Imagining India, its dense deep fragrance in my nos-
> trils, the jungle before me, unknown, perhaps unknowable, I thought of
> this southern sky of which I had read: studded with strange stars and
> bewildering asterisms: none of them familiar to us; and yet a whole civili-
> zation, many civilizations, had steered their boats looking up and orien-
> tating themselves from this totally different pattern.[38]

In contrast to his academic colleagues who emphasized philology and
the literal translation of texts, Zimmer sought to understand the meaning behind the words and to integrate the truth he found in Indian
material with the accepted truths of the West. Writing of this material,

[37] Hegel is discussed by Willson, *A Mythical Image*, 117–20, and Mitter, *Much Maligned
Monsters*, 208–19.

[38] Zimmer, *Artistic Form and Yoga*, 248.

he commented that "the task was to transmute it so as to make it fit into the context of our own experiences and traditions: a process of mutual transmutation, assimilation."[39] The study of Indian texts was for Zimmer a personal as well as intellectual quest.

Zimmer was not unaware of the controversies surrounding India and art history, although there is no indication in his biographical notes or in his early writings that he knew of the intricacies of the debates in England confronting Coomaraswamy. He thought that art historical methodology isolated art, deprived it "of roots in real soil." Indeed, Zimmer eventually wrote *Kunstform und Yoga im indischen Kultbild* (1926) to do away with "the then prevailing purely esthetic approach to Indian art on the one hand, and with the barren classistic criticism on the other."[40] It should be noted that when Zimmer wrote this book, Coomaraswamy had not yet written at length on art theory, and what was published in Germany probably had a limited circulation in England and America. Despite disparate backgrounds, then, Zimmer and Coomaraswamy perceived identical goals and independently drew on texts to comprehend the inner meaning of Indian art. And perhaps not surprisingly, they came to similar observations.

Zimmer enumerated three major influences on his thinking: the Tantric texts that were edited and published by Sir John Woodroffe in Europe in the 1910s, the Puranas (compendia of Indian mythological and historical traditions that he studied to a degree unprecedented in Europe), and Carl Jung's *Psychology of the Unconscious*.[41] The Tantras, a corpus of esoteric literature, reveal the role that sacred images, particularly Shaivite images, play in religious life and the meaning attached to the images, as well as elucidating magical rites. Between 1918 and 1924 Zimmer studied the eight Tantric texts published by Woodroffe and in 1926 presented his penetrating analysis of the meaning and instrumentality of Indian images as meditational devices in *Kunstform und Yoga*. With this publication Zimmer delved to the core of the metaphysics of Indian imagery with a clarity and breadth of understanding that was probably never rivaled even by Coomaraswamy.

Zimmer began the answer to his basic question—"Why is so prominent a phenomenon of Indian art as the sacred image, in its most basic

[39] Ibid., 256–57.

[40] Ibid., 255.

[41] Ibid., 259. Sir John Woodroffe, who sometimes used the pseudonym Arthur Avalon, edited and published Tantric texts and also wrote books interpreting them. For the original texts, see Arthur Avalon, *Tantrik Texts*, 8 vols. (London: Luzac & Co., 1913–1918). One of the interpretive works that Zimmer probably read was Sir John Woodroffe, *Śakti and Śakta* (1918; 6th ed., Madras: Ganesh & Co., 1965). See also C. G. Jung, *Psychology of the Unconscious*, trans. Beatrice M. Hickle (New York: Dodd, Mead, 1925).

formal structure, constituted the way it is?"—with a descriptive juxta-position of classical and Indian sculpture. Classical art captures one moment in time and is rich in relationships of parts to one another, a characteristic that prompts the gaze to move in a circular fashion, eventually encompassing the entire work. Indian sculpture, by con-trast, is still, at rest, oblivious to the viewer; it can be seen as a single unit that captures the essence of being, rather than one moment in time.

The Tantras provide the key to the spiritual world in which Hindu deities are rooted. The world is an unfolding of divine, feminine en-ergy (*shakti*) into a world rich in manifestations; *shakti* is conscious-ness, a blissful state of being equal to *brahman*, being-not-yet-unfolded. *Shakti* is endowed with the power of *maya* (illusion) and because of this, unfolding from the state of not-yet-unfolded, can transform itself into the form of a god or goddess possessing attributes. Pure being in its first transformation from its not-yet-unfolded state reveals itself as the divine couple Shiva and Shakti: they are one under the two aspects of repose-in-itself and the energy that unfolds itself. This theme of ap-parent, but nonexistent, duality, is central to Zimmer's subsequent analysis of Indian thought and interpretation of artistic expression.

Pure spiritual being, however, strives to return to the undifferenti-ated state in human and divine consciousness; man wishes to experi-ence himself as *brahman*, to experience pure consciousness, to feel it and himself as one and the same, that is, divine. This is the ultimate goal of devotional practice: for the perceiver and perceived to become one and for dualistic consciousness to end. The path to this goal is worship (*puja*) of images, which involves yogic practices. The degree to which the devotee is successful depends on technical ability and maturity.

A sacred image is a tool or representational device, a *yantra*, that is made the focus of magical and ritual spiritual functions. These *yantras* may be figurative (images, *pratima*), auditory (sacred syllables, *man-tras*), or linear, either with figurative or written symbols or purely geo-metric in form. The forms are congruent in ritual function but are or-dered in a hierarchy of decreasing significance from purely geometric to figurative. The spiritual activity of the devotee gives significance to the *yantra*. In the first stage, the devotee produces in his own inner being a visualization of divine essence and then projects it upon the sacred image placed before him. Preliminary to this is purification of the area of devotion and of the ritual devices, after which the devotee proceeds to *mantras*, gestures, and breathing exercises to arouse the divine nature of the body. Proceeding to meditation (*dhyana*), the dev-otee constructs the image of the god's essential nature before continuing to the external *puja*, in which he breathes his energy (*tejas*) into flowers and touches the flowers to the image, thereby establishing the god in the image. The rituals subsequently performed allow the devotee to experience himself as the divine. At this point the second stage occurs: the energy unfolded plunges back into the state of enfolded being.

Because *yantras*, especially figurative images (*pratima*), are accurate copies of supernatural essences, they must correspond exactly to the deity of the heart visualized in detail in meditation, which is then projected onto the *yantra*. Thus, the *yantra* must conform absolutely to canonical prescriptions. It is the vessel and replication of the inner vision. In meditation, the visualization fills up the entire field of vision and each detail is seen at once; the vision juxtaposes essential signs that must appear together to be a complete reproduction of supernatural essence. This is why Indian sculpture is seen as a single unit and does not invite eye movement. There is, moreover, no room for any decorative fashioning on the artist's part; the *yantra* must be free from individual capriciousness. Three factors ensure the accuracy of the repertoire of symbolic signs of the *yantra*: the literary tradition of myths that preserve descriptions of deities' appearances, traditions of artistic craftsmanship that pass from father to son, and previous models handed down as standardized representations. All that is left to the artist is the quality of artistic execution.

To assure the fidelity of the image to the inner vision, canons of proportions and a language of signs (iconography) particular to images are provided in the Puranas and other specialized texts.[42] Because *yantras* are diagrams of esoteric symbols, they are more analogous to scientific formulas than to artistic creations of individualistic genius. Indian imagery appears static and still because it is geometrically determined by a theory of proportion that regulates the relative size of figures within a composition (based on a hierarchy of importance) and predetermines the algebraically calculated size of the body parts of a single figure.

Zimmer also elaborates on the geometric, symmetrical *mandalas* of Tibetan Buddhism as linear *yantra* that are "road maps" of truth: of the unfolding of the emptiness from the center to the realm of *maya*, the phenomonal world at the periphery, and of the enfolding back to the center. A *mandala* decorated with figures or written signs is a mosaic of symbols. The rituals for visualization in Buddhism are similar to those of Hinduism, and the mandala is homologous in function to a Hindu *yantra*, whether figurative or linear. And, with a flash of genius,

---

[42] Zimmer consulted the *Vishnudharmottara*, pt. 3, and the *Citralakshana*.

Zimmer recognized that the *stupa* at Borobudur was "the most im-
pressive mandala the art of Buddhism has ever created in the visible
world as a symbol of its truth."[43] The concentric galleries of the structure represent stages of increasing consciousness as the pilgrim as-
cends and progresses to the center, until, at the apex of the *stupa*, the
devotee experiences his divine essence.[44] Remarkably, Zimmer never
realized that a Hindu temple was also a three-dimensional *mandala*.

In *Kunstform und Yoga*, Zimmer described, as no one else had before,
the Indian metaphysical worldview or conceptual framework within
which Hindu and Buddhist images were produced and the instrumentality of these images for meditation. Other original contributions were
his explanations of the unfolding and enfolding process by which the
devotee experienced the divine in himself and thus resolved the duality of the I and Not-I, the equivalence and hierarchy of *yantra* types,
and the homology of *mandalas* and three-dimensional architecture. As
did Coomaraswamy, Zimmer recognized that art and religion were inseparable—indeed, art represents the divine through iconography—
that images are visualizations by the worshiper, and that iconography
and the proportions of images are determined by tradition.

Coomaraswamy, who pursued themes presented by Havell on the
idealism of Indian art and the need to understand the intention of the
artist, recognized the profoundity of Zimmer's work.[45] To understand
Indian art as the maker and user did was central to his commentary to
his Western audience. According to Coomaraswamy, given Zimmer's
exposition of the instrumentality of Hindu imagery, no longer could
the study of nature be the basis for interpreting stylistic sequences, and
now that "why it is what it is" was understood and accepted, it was
possible to trace stylistic sequences in time and place as records of cultural and spiritual movement. Coomaraswamy seemed to imply that
Zimmer's work was the final statement on the metaphysics and aesthetics of Indian art and had established "spiritual movement" as the
basis for style.

I would like to return to Coomaraswamy's theory of art and the role
of artists in traditional society in publications subsequent to *Mediaeval
Sinhalese Art* to trace his theoretical development and to evaluate the
impact Zimmer's work had on his own. He published three books—
The Indian Craftsman (1909), *The Arts and Crafts of India and Ceylon*

---

[43] Zimmer, *Artistic Form and Yoga*, 114.

[44] As Gerald Chapple and James B. Lawson noted in the preface to *Artistic Form and
Yoga* (xix), this analysis influenced the work of Paul Mus. Mus's discussion of Zimmer's
interpretation is in "Barabudur," *Bulletin de l'Ecole Francaise d'Extrême-Orient* 32 (1932):
320–23.

[45] Coomaraswamy, *Artibus Asiae* 4, no. 1 (1930–32): 78–79.

(1913), and the *History of Indian and Indonesian Art* (1927)—that in fact present little of his theory beyond that contained in his first book, although the second continued metaphysical speculations mentioned in *Mediaeval Sinhalese Art*.[46] It must be remembered that Coomaraswamy accepted a priori that traditional society was "normal" and that traditional culture anywhere in the world was equivalent to that of medieval Europe. His writings increasingly relied on Western sources, particularly Meister Eckhart, to explain his views and expose the "abnormality" of contemporary culture. There is a tendency also in his theoretical articles to refer more to "art" and less to particular objects. In other words, his ideas became contructs from texts, less and less informed by direct observation. As much as possible, I will use Coomaraswamy's own words to convey the incremental complexity of his thought on his primary themes.

In *The Dance of Śiva* (1924) Coomaraswamy elaborated on the view that art was produced through yogic practices. The process was the same for worshiper and artist, who in texts is termed equally *shilpin*, *yogi*, or *sadhaka*. During meditation, the divinity appeared to the artist as if in a dream, and the brilliant image became the artist's model. In contrast to the worshiper, the artist would then proceed to represent the mental picture in objective form.[47] In other words, the work of art was completed before the representation was begun. Myth, dream, and art were one and represented man's innermost hopes and fears. The artist obeyed a hierarchic canon and did not view his work from an aesthetic point of view but as that of a pious artisan to whom the theme was all important. Beauty is what we "do to" a work of art, rather than a quality present in the object.

Coomaraswamy put forward significantly more substantial observations in *The Transformation of Nature in Art* (1934), and these reveal reliance on Zimmer's scholarship. In Asian tradition the mind of the artist visualizes the canonically prescribed form of the god as though from a great distance—from heaven, where the types of art exist in formal operation. These types or prototypes are "those of sentient activity or functional utility conceivable only in a contingent world."[48] Coomaraswamy suggests that nature is what is made intelligible by the artist through iconography, which consists of signs (abbreviated expressions of something known) and symbols (allusions to something

[46] Ananda K. Coomaraswamy, *The Arts and Crafts of India and Ceylon* (1913; repr. New York: Noonday Press, 1964).

[47] Ananda K. Coomaraswamy, *The Dance of Śiva* (1924; repr. New York: Dover, 1985), 22.

[48] Ananda K. Coomaraswamy, *The Transformation of Nature in Art* (1934; repr. New York: Dover, 1956), 17.

unknown, but acknowledged to exist). Because the artist uses a mental construct and not models in nature, the art is cerebral in character.

Having established these distinctions, Coomaraswamy then described the pecularities of Oriental art in terms that incorporated Zimmer's ideas and specific vocabulary:

> The Indian icon is ... a visual symbolism. ... The "anthropomorphic" icon is of the same kind as a *yantra*, that is, a geometrical representation of the deity, or a *mantra*, that is, an auditory representation of the deity. ... The Indian icon fills the whole field of vision at once, all is equally clear and equally essential; the eye is not led to range from one point to another, as in empirical vision, nor to seek a concentration of meaning in one part more than another. ... The parts of the icon are not organically related, for it is not contemplated that they should function biologically, but ideally related. ... The relation is mental rather than functional.[49]

This was, in fact, a summary of *Kunstform und Yoga* that was taken verbatim from his review of Zimmer's book. Elsewhere in *The Transformation of Nature in Art*, Coomaraswamy, describing the process of worship, follows Zimmer's formulation: yoga leads to identity of consciousness with the desired object (deity) through the use of trance *mantras*, flowers and offerings are made, and the deity is worshiped as the self.[50]

The process of unfolding into the phenomonal world and enfolding back to the absolute during yoga that Zimmer identified is also woven into Coomaraswamy's later works. In describing once again, but in greater detail, the process of meditation by which the artist visualizes the deity to be made, Coomaraswamy states that once the vision is complete, the artist returns to himself.[51] Likewise, he recognized that the Hindu temple was a three-dimensional *mandala* and applied Zimmer's analysis of the structure of Tibetan *mandalas* and their function in meditation to the form and function of the temple:

> The temple is the universe in a likeness, its dark interior is occupied by a single image or symbol of the informing Spirit, while externally its walls are covered with representations of the Divine Powers in all their manifested multiplicity. ... One proceeds inwards from multiplicity to unity, just as in contemplation; and on returning again to the outer world, one sees ... all the innumerable forms that the Agent within assumes in his playful activity.[52]

[49] Ibid., 63.
[50] Ibid., 164.
[51] Ananda K. Coomaraswamy, *Why Exhibit Works of Art?* (London: Luzac & Co., 1943), 37.
[52] "An Indian Temple: The Kandarya Mahadeo," in Lipsey, ed., *Coomaraswamy*, 1:10.

Coomaraswamy does not footnote Zimmer's work in these passages; it seems probable that Zimmer's insights had resonated so closely with Coomaraswamy's own thinking that the two were no longer distinguishable. To put it another way, Zimmer's ideas did not so much transform Coomaraswamy's thoughts as provide a broader metaphysical framework for them and lend a greater authority to his elaborations.

Did Coomaraswamy's work have a strong impact on Zimmer's thinking subsequent to *Kunstform und Yoga*? None of Zimmer's scholarly publications that I have read indicate this. After the publication of *Kunstform und Yoga*, Zimmer began to study the Puranas extensively, and from 1932 onward he sought to combine myth and psychology in order to understand Indian thought. The only possible acknowledgment of Coomaraswamy's work may be Zimmer's choice of themes to be elaborated on while teaching. One example may be the extensive analysis of the lotus published in *The Art of Indian Asia*. Coomaraswamy had stated that the lotus was significant in Indian art in *Mediaeval Sinhalese Art*; Zimmer also recognized this in *Kunstform und Yoga*. In 1931 Coomaraswamy published a study on *yakshas* (nature spirits) that established the association of these spirits, as well as the lotus, the *makara* (a quasi-crocodilian creature), overflowing pots, and river goddesses, with water cosmology.[53] Coomaraswamy offered a more extensive analysis of the lotus in *Elements of Buddhist Iconography* (1935). But, even if Zimmer was aware of these writings, in characteristic fashion he discussed the lotus symbol in *The Art of Indian Asia* and in *Myths and Symbols in Indian Art and Civilization* in the context of his own observations based on the Puranas. Moreover, three other equally prominent themes of *The Art of Indian Asia*—the archetypal mother goddess, ideals of Indian feminine beauty, and the theme of the unity of opposites—were pure Zimmer. Zimmer's comment that Coomaraswamy was a source of inspiration to him may have referred to Coomaraswamy's specialized writings, but it is not obvious that he incorporated specific information from them in his lecture notes. Indeed, Zimmer may have been referring solely to Coomaraswamy's *History of Indian and Indonesian Art*, which had been in circulation since 1927 and was therefore available to Zimmer from an early date, and which he ultimately used as a text.

How successful was either Zimmer or Coomaraswamy in making Indian art more understandable? Essentially, neither attempted to refute head-on the criticisms of Indian art as expressed by Birdwood in 1910,

[53] Ananda K. Coomaraswamy, *Yakṣas*, pt. 2 (Washington, D.C.: Freer Gallery of Art, 1931), 1–84.

for both understood those criticisms to be founded on a misconception. Rather, each argued that Indian art should be evaluated by its own standards, which were different from those of the West. To this end, each explained in great detail the characteristics, production, and function of Indian art to confirm that it was utilitarian and that its form was predetermined by canonical prescriptions—to assure an iconographically correct reproduction of an inner vision. Moreover, divine essence, rather than nature, was the content of this inner vision. In describing these characteristics of Indian art, each surely succeeded.

Coomaraswamy subsequently went on to say that the measure of the quality of a sculpture produced in traditional society was the degree to which it conformed to the artist's inner vision. As Mitter has pointed out, since no one other than the artist could know the content of this inner vision, Coomaraswamy's stance eliminated any objective criteria by which to evaluate Indian art and thus foreclosed any attempt to describe Indian art in concrete, nonmetaphysical terms.[54] Not only were objective criteria lacking but even the vocabulary employed by Coomaraswamy and Zimmer reinforced negative Western judgments. Terms such as *magical*, *dream*, and *vision* unfortunately served to maintain the stereotype of the irrationality of Indian art prevalent in both English and German scholarship. In much the same way, the emphasis on the fidelity of the artisan to tradition reinforced the perceived lack of creativity among Indian artists and the static character of their art.

Neither Zimmer nor Coomaraswamy addressed this problem directly. There is certainly no denying the instrumentality of images for meditation, that images represent the divine, or that images were made according to iconographic and proportional canons. Even within these parameters, however, there is evidence of formal and iconographic innovation in Indian art over the centuries. But Zimmer merely says that tradition determines the formal elements in an image; these elements are constant to type but vary depending upon the era and geographical area.[55] Coomaraswamy states, somewhat vaguely, that human idiosyncrasy—something of the artist—is responsible for style.[56] But these ideas are never reconciled with the major premise in their works: that the image is a replication of an inner visualization of immutable divine essence. The question is, following their logic, How was the original image, which was then handed down from generation

[54] Mitter, *Much Maligned Monsters*, 283.
[55] Zimmer, *Artistic Form and Yoga*, 53.
[56] Coomaraswamy, *Why Exhibit Works of Art?* 39.

to generation, formulated? And, if the divine is immutable, what or who is responsible for subsequent changes in imagery? These are the most significant questions that both neglected.

By emphasizing exclusive reliance on metaphysical experience as the basis for artistic expression, both Coomaraswamy and Zimmer, like their less sympathetic contemporaries, denied the Indian artisan the capacity to exercise a rational decision-making process. Indeed, this was as true of the "transcendentalists" as it was of the "archeologists," who simply neglected the human element. Coomaraswamy states that the artist visualizes the image "as if in a dream," which implies nonrational, uncontrolled activity. Zimmer is somewhat more ambiguous about the meditative activity of the artist but states emphatically that the image must be an exact replica of the inner vision (as determined by tradition) and free from individual capriciousness. There is no room for innovation or personal interpretation. In so earnestly attempting to establish that the criteria for judging Indian art should be different from those for Western art, both neglected issues that could have added greater nuance and depth to their arguments.

It seems reasonable to argue that Zimmer and Coomaraswamy largely failed to consider human agency because both assumed the primacy of texts. Consulting texts per se is not inappropriate, but both depended on this source to the neglect of more extensive observation of an equally important primary source: sculptures and temples in context. Coomaraswamy did travel in India, but in his writings there are few descriptions of the formal characteristics of sculpture or temples. From his initial publication in 1908 until his last works in 1947, there is a decrease in discussion of the actual art and a corresponding expansion of textual references. His theoretical writings, as mentioned above, became constructs from texts and were less and less the result of direct observation. Zimmer's contextual experience was limited to viewing sculptures in museums and in photographs, and his observations of architecture were based solely on photographs. As Kramrisch noted in her review, Zimmer's response was to the mythological content, rather than the formal characteristics, of the art.

The fact remains, though, that iconography did change through the centuries, as did symbols. By insisting on the primacy of texts, which both Coomaraswamy and Zimmer interpreted as expressing the unchanging, eternal divine, neither could explain the development of a particular form or account for regional variations on it except in vague generalities. Precisely because artifactual material can be situated in time and place—as texts often cannot—they are a more faithful recording of development and transmutations enacted by human agents even within prescribed parameters. Greater understanding of artifactual material would have made that human element more obvious. This might in turn not only have led them to question the absolute authority of the textual tradition but also have expanded the scope of inquiry to present more substantive answers to European criticisms.

Another primary source was recognized, but neglected, by Coomaraswamy: living artisans. He had consulted a Kandyan artisan when writing *Mediaeval Sinhalese Art*,[57] and even as late as 1927 he called for a detailed study of the methods of building a modern Hindu temple in Tamil Nadu, where the Kammalar caste was still active.[58] Curiously, though, he abandoned the use of contemporary artisans as informants after the 1908 volume. Informants could have shed light on the human element in the making of Indian art and could have described with a richness of detail not available in cryptic texts the complexity of the artistic process. But as Coomaraswamy delved into theory, which caused him to glorify the past and to reject the present (an involution that in fact justified his rejection of the present), he concluded that in the colonial period Hindus no longer understood their own art.[59] One promising direction in his early work thus never bore fruit.

The role and practice of the artist and the degree of innovation throughout the history of Indian art are essential topics that are now beginning to be explored with the participation of practicing artisans.[60] When these issues are better understood, it may be possible to develop a more complex and culturally sensitive understanding of Indian art and theory. A more thorough understanding of the production of art in the South Asian context should consider the primary sources mentioned above, texts and artisans, as well as a third, the patron. Texts transmit tradition; the architect/artisan embodies that tradition by learning and practice and is the agent of production; and the patron is the activator of what may be termed a dialogical process that results in the construction of a temple with an iconographic program that explicates a chosen theology.[61] Each primary source participates in the dia-

[57] Coomaraswamy, *Medieval Sinhalese Art*, xi.

[58] Coomaraswamy, *History of Indian and Indonesian Art* (1927; repr. New York: Dover, 1965), 125.

[59] Coomaraswamy, *Artibus Asiae* 4, no. 1 (1930–32): 79.

[60] Joanna Williams, "Criticizing and Evaluating the Visual Arts in India: A Preliminary Example," *Journal of Asian Studies* 47, no. 1 (February 1988): 3–28; Frederick Asher, "On Stone and Artistic Production," in *Aspects of India*, ed. Margaret Case and N. Gerald Barrier (New Delhi: American Institute of Indian Studies, 1986), 63–68; John F. Mosteller, "The Problem of Proportion and Style in Indian Art History: Or Why All Buddhas in Fact Do Not Look Alike," *Art Journal* 49, no. 4 (Winter 1990): 388–94.

[61] In suggesting this, I am relying on Bakhtin's analysis of the novel as dialogical discourse. See the chapter on "Discourse in the Novel" in M. M. Bakhtin, *The Dialogic Imagination*, ed. Michael Holquist, trans. Caryl Emerson and Michael Holquist (Austin: University of Texas Press, 1981), 259–422.

logue; each contributes knowledge, experience, and a set of expectations, or individual "vocabularies," to the language of the discourse that results in the temple and its associated imagery.

For those of us in the present analyzing the past, the formal and iconographic elements of each temple and sculpture, and the chronological development of these same elements, afford another primary source to be considered in addition to texts, artisans/architects (names, castes, guilds) and patrons/donors (name, status, sectarian beliefs). Once completed, the temple and associated icons constituted one element of a local or regional tradition, referred to and expanded on by subsequent architects and artisans. In studying the past, the artifactual material itself is a source, not just a product, of discourse.

The totality of the "discourse is dialogical" theory expands the dimensions of the inquiry beyond that of texts and a limited number of artifacts to include social and human factors. Metaphysics expounded in texts would then be only one factor among several to describe in more concrete terms why Indian art "is the way it is."

Such considerations notwithstanding, understood within their cultural and intellectual contexts Zimmer and Coomaraswamy remain two of the Promethian interpreters of Indian art of the twentieth century. Each passionately and intelligently explicated his perspectives on the subject. Despite what seems in retrospect to be the limitations of their work, they were among the first, and were certainly the most articulate, of those who attempted to understand Indian art on its own terms.

CONTRIBUTORS

MARGARET H. CASE, a freelance editor and writer, is a consulting editor at Princeton University Press, where she was for many years Asian Studies editor.

GERALD CHAPPLE is Associate Professor of German at McMaster University in Hamilton, Ontario. He has translated or edited seven books, the latest a co-translation of *The Convent School* by the contemporary Austrian writer Barbara Frischmuth (Riverside, Calif.: Ariadne Press, 1993).

WENDY DONIGER is the Mircea Eliade Professor of the History of Religions at the University of Chicago. She is the author of numerous books on Indian mythology under the name of Wendy Doniger O'Flaherty, including *Asceticism and Eroticism in the Mythology of Siva* (London: Oxford University Press, 1973), *Hindu Myths* (Baltimore: Penguin, 1975), and *Women, Androgynes, and Other Mythical Beasts* (Chicago: University of Chicago Press, 1980). Most recently, she translated Yves Bonnefoy's two-volume *Mythologies* (Chicago: University of Chicago Press, 1991).

MATTHEW KAPSTEIN teaches philosophy of religion at Columbia University. Among his publications is the English edition of Dudjom Rimpoche, *The Nyingma School of Tibetan Buddhism: Its Fundamentals and History*, 2 vols. (Boston: Wisdom Publications, 1991), of which he is co-translator.

JAMES B. LAWSON is Associate Professor of German at McMaster University in Hamilton, Ontario. His third work of co-translation, Barbara Frischmuth's novel *The Convent School*, appeared in 1993; he is currently translating some of Frischmuth's more recent writings.

MARY F. LINDA is Assistant Director of the Palmer Museum of Art at Pennsylvania State University. She has published several articles in *Artibus Asiae* and *Ars Orientalis*, and edited *The Real, the Fake and the Masterpiece* (New York: Asia Society, 1988).

WILLIAM MCGUIRE, an editor of the Bollingen Series for some forty years, is the author of *Bollingen: An Adventure in Collecting the Past* (Princeton: Princeton University Press, 1982).

MAYA RAUCH, born in 1925 in Heidelberg, studied philosophy at Zurich, where she taught until 1987. She is now managing Heinrich Zimmer's literary estate.

KENNETH G. ZYSK is Professor of Religious Studies at New York University and author of *Asceticism and Healing in Ancient India* (London: Oxford University Press, 1991).

INDEX

Esslinger, Eugen, 15
Esslinger-Rauch, Mila, 15, 16

Froebe-Kapteyn, Olga, 31, 32, 37, 39

garlic, 94
Glasenapp, Helmut von, 62
Goethe, Johann Wolfgang von, 23, 28, 71n

Hamlet, 84–85
Hastyayurveda, 88, 94
Hauer, J. W., 32
Hauschild, Richard, 67n
Havell, E. B., 125–27, 134
Hegel, Georg Wilhelm Friedrich, 11, 25, 69, 71n; on Indian art, 130; on Oriental philosophy, 108
Heidegger, Martin, 109n
Heidelberg, 7, 38; center of German romanticism, 25, 75
Heidelberg University: Nazis dismiss faculty, 73; Zimmer dismissed from, 17, 21, 28, 30, 33, 72; Zimmer teaches at, 15, 16, 21, 73
Henderson, Helena, 37
Henderson, Joseph, 37
Herder, Johann, Gottfried, 129
Hofmannsthal, Hugo von, 16, 28, 42, 68
Hofmannsthal, Raimund, 33, 74
humors (*dosha*), 89, 96, 100, 101
Husserl, Edmund, 111

I Ching, 34, 38, 41

Jaspers, Karl, 59n
jaundice, 91
Johns Hopkins University, Zimmer lectures at, 34, 74, 87–103
Jones, Owen, 124n
Joyce, James, 33, 53, 75–76
Jung, Carl Gustav, 25; in America, 37; and Campbell, 3; at Eranos, 32; in India, 10–12; influence on Zimmer, 3, 7–11, 131; meets Mellons, 31; opinion of Zimmer, 42; as Zen master, 43–47; Zimmer dedicates book to, 73; Zimmer's opinion of, 43–47, 71
Jung Club. *See* Analytical Psychology Club
Jung Foundation, 50
Jungfrauen, die, 50, 71

King, Jeff, 39, 40
Kitagawa, Joseph, 53n
Kommerell, Max, 27
Kracauer, Siegfried, 84
Kramrisch, Stella, 13, 81n; works, 123; and Zimmer, 119–20, 122

Laping, Johannes, 100
Lawrence, Frieda, 37
Lehmann, Karl, 38, 41, 42
Lehmann, Phyllis Williams, 41
Lehmann-Haupt, Hellmut, 39
Leisegang, Hans, 32
Lipsey, Roger, 41
Losch, Hans, 72n
lotus symbol, 119, 137
Lüders, Heinrich, 4, 63, 68, 110
luta spider, 94

Manasa, 93, 94
mandalas, 46, 112, 133–34; Borobudur as, 134; temple as, 136; Tibetan, 136
Mann, Thomas, 56, 79–80
Massignon, Louis, 32, 33
Matilal, Bimal K., 106, 107
maya, 24–26, 114, 116, 132
medicine, Indian: anatomy in, 95, 98; Ayurveda, 90, 92, 93, 95, 96, 101; of body and soul, 89, 96; dissection in, 98–99; fees in, 92; Greek interaction with, 99–101; healing plants in, 91–93; "magical," 90–94; materia medica of, 90, 99, 100; and philosophy, 109; romantic aspect of, 96–97; spiritual goal of, 89, 95
Mellon, Mary, 13, 31–34, 37; at Bollingen, 33; death, 91; educates Zimmer's sons, 40; and Zimmer, 33, 34, 42. *See also* Bollingen Series
Mellon, Paul, 13, 31–33, 37; at Bollingen, 33; continues Bollingen Series, 41; educates Zimmer's sons, 40; establishes Old Dominion Foundation, 38
Meulenbeld, J. Jan, 101
Morris, William, 124
Mountain Lake, 37
Mus, Paul, 134n
myth(s): and dreams, 25, 44, 58, 71; Greek, 56; Jung's knowledge of, 44; as "romance of the soul," 45; as social history, 45; and truth, 24–26; and transforma-